I0805320

Printed in the United States
by Baker & Taylor Publisher Services

A Messianic Jewish Haggadah for Passover

A Translation by

Rabbi Barry A. Budoff

ר' בצלאל אברם בן־יעקב הלוי, זצ"ל

Edited by

Rabbi Kirk Gliebe

ר' שאול בן־יוסף

Editorial Committee:

Dr. Michael Gabizon, Rabbi David Katz, Rabbi Dr. Daniel Nessim

Illustrations by

Elisa Mattson

First Edition: March 8, 2024

Published by:

Devar Emet Messianic Publications
7800 Niles Avenue; Skokie, IL 60077
847-674-9146
www.demjo.org

ISBN: 979-8-9878279-1-8

Note: all verse references follow traditional Jewish Scriptural verse numbering

Illustrations adapted from the following historic Haggadahs:
Prato Haggadah, Spain, 1300
Birds' Head Haggadah, Germany, 1300
Barcelona Haggadah, Spain, 1340
Sarajevo Haggadah, Spain 1350
Lombard Haggadah, Italy 1390
Amsterdam Haggadah, Netherlands, 1695
Passover Haggadah, Germany 1740
Darmstadt Pessach Haggadah, Denmark, 1769
Bouton Haggadah, 1870

Table of Contents:

The Development of Passover: From Temple to Table

Jewish families around the world celebrate Passover as a night of remembrance: of God's redemption of our ancestors from Egypt, of our struggles throughout Jewish history, and of God's promise of ultimate redemption for Israel when Messiah comes. The Scriptural story of Passover provides for us a clear theological and religious understanding of God's active part in Jewish history. This documentation of history helps us understand how God has kept the Jewish people, against all odds, until this very day.

The development of the Passover traditions that we follow as Jewish people are not as clearly understood, nor are quite as old, as many think. **Seder** means ***order***, **Haggadah** means ***story***, and the holiday of Passover as celebrated today, with its procedures, narrative, foods, customs and songs, are mostly recent developments since the Middle Ages (5th to 15th centuries of the Common Era). In this introduction to the Budoff Haggadah, we explore the Scriptural backgrounds for Passover, as well as present an overview of the development of the modern Seder. If you wish to study this more deeply, we suggest you turn to the Bibliography section at the back of this Haggadah for a list of books and articles regarding Passover and the seder's development.

The Scriptures clearly teach that God delivered the descendants of Abraham, Isaac and Jacob from Egyptian slavery by His intentional effort. Exodus 12 and 13 are the first and most formative texts recounting this effort, and they include the details and items required to celebrate the annual remembrance of the event: a lamb, bitter herbs and unleavened bread, with the lamb as the central element. The event was to be celebrated each year on a specific night, the 15th of Nisan, starting off a seven-day holiday called the Festival of Matsah (Unleavened Bread), requiring Israel to remove all leavened products חָמֵץ *(ḥameits)* from their possession. As the Hebrew text relates in Exodus 12:42, the 15th of Nisan is a special night of vigil by God for His Jewish people, and remains so until our day. When Jewish people set aside and celebrate Passover on this night, we experience a special connection with God; He is with us and our people like no other night of the year!

The Hebrew Scriptures describe Passover and the Festival of Matsah with varying degrees of detail (Exodus 23:15, Leviticus 23:5-8, Numbers 9:1-14, Deuteronomy 16:1-8). Unfortunately, the Scriptures also relate that the people rarely actually celebrated the holiday during the times of the Kings (Joshua 5:10-11; 2 Kings 23:21-23, 2 Chronicles 35:1-19), although in Ezekiel 45:21-23 Passover is mentioned as being celebrated in the future Kingdom of Messiah.

Few details remain in surviving Second Temple period literature about how the Jewish people celebrated Passover. The Scriptures and other Jewish literature written before 100 CE (Jubilees, Philo and Josephus) convey the joyfulness of the celebration; the sacrifice of the lamb on the 14th of Nisan in the afternoon and the mandatory eating of the roasted lamb after sundown in Jerusalem while in groups of at least ten; the drinking of wine and the eating of matsah, bitter herbs and possibly ḥaroset as part of the celebratory meal; and the singing of the Hallel Psalms at the Temple by the Levitical priests. However, no specific order for the meal is clearly given in any of these texts. The B'rit Ḥadashah *(New Testament)* references to Passover mention most of these elements as well (Matthew 26:17-30, Mark 14:12-26, Luke 22:7-30, John 2:13-25, John 13:1-30).

Yeshua's last Passover with his talmidim seems to assume an existing order to their meal, but no specific order is clearly presented. A clear order is found only after the Temple's destruction, in the Rabbinic literature of the late second century CE in the Mishnah and Tosefta. The reason for this seems to be related to efforts by the Rabbis to bring the religious practices of the destroyed Temple into the individual homes of the Jewish community. This was done not only to strengthen the religious practice and covenant commitment of the community, but also to focus the attention of the surviving Jewish people away from the horrific losses in their recent history to a new hope and future without Temple worship. This effort to bring the sanctity and practices of the Jerusalem Temple to the average Jewish dining table is well documented within Rabbinic literature. It strengthened both the faith and identity of the Jewish people as they sought to live on as God's Chosen People without their land and without their traditional religious center.

This Messianic Jewish Haggadah follows the traditional format and customs of the Ashkenazi Jewish community, reflecting our own families' European Jewish backgrounds. Some sections of text have been edited to shorten the length of the Haggadah. In a few places, we have added unique elements from non-Ashkenazi traditions that seem to be older than our own, and that shed light on the mindset of those who originally set in motion the development of the Seder meal. Nevertheless, it is our hope that all members of the Jewish community, regardless of their family background, will find the Budoff Haggadah to be both meaningful and useful for their own Seder.

This Messianic Jewish Haggadah also reflects our faith in the Messiah of Israel, Yeshua. As a result, some traditional blessings, statements and portions of texts have been slightly amended, and we have added texts from the B'rit Ḥadashah. Messiah Yeshua presented himself at his last Passover meal with his talmidim as Israel's ultimate Passover Lamb. He built on the redemptive lamb of our Egyptian Exodus, and pointed towards his provision of a greater redemption through the sacrifice of his life to bring full and complete forgiveness of sin for anyone who would accept him. Even with these additions, you will find that we have still maintained the traditional flow of the Haggadah.

It is our hope that this Haggadah will both remind us as Jewish people of our national and historic journey from Egypt to freedom, and encourage us as individual Jews in our personal and spiritual journey from sin to freedom through faith in our ultimate Passover Lamb, Messiah Yeshua.

How to Use this Haggadah

Those desiring a full, traditional Seder experience can read through the Budoff Haggadah in its entirety, which will take several hours to complete, including dinner of course. Those needing to plan for a shorter Seder can follow the on the bottom of key pages to focus on the main points of the Haggadah.

Hebrew Transliteration Guide:

Hebrew Consonants	Transliteration	Sound
ח	ḥ (see dot below "h")	**Ch**anuka
ךְ,ך,כ	kh	Baru**kh**
ךּ,כּ	k	**K**ippa
שׁ	sh	**Sh**abbat
שׂ	s	**S**amuel
צ,ץ	ts	**Ts'**daka
ה	h	**H**alleluya

Hebrew Vowels	Transliteration	Sound
אָ	a	**Awe**
אַ	a	**A**pple
אִ	i	B**ee**
אֵ	ei	L**ay**
אֶ	e	B**e**d
אֹ or וֹ	o	R**o**w
אֻ or וּ	u	B**oot**
אְ	sometimes e or sometimes ' like b**e**d. When silent or ending a syllable it is a '.	

Preparing the Home for Passover

In preparation for Passover, all foods considered to be ḥameits need to be removed from one's home. According to the Scriptural instruction, this specifically means that any foods containing yeast must be either thrown out or given away. There are numerous additional items considered to be ḥameits according to Jewish tradition which vary by community custom. These consist of food items containing corn syrup, legumes or grains not considered kosher for Passover. The determination of what is considered ḥameits beyond items with yeast specifically needs to be considered on an individual basis according to community custom and in consultation with community Rabbis.

Bedikat Ḥameits

(After sundown on the 14th of Nisan, the night before Passover, a ceremonial search for any final ḥameits is done in the home using a candle, a feather and a wooden spoon, to ceremonially remove ḥameits after the reciting of the following blessing)

בָּרוּךְ אַתָּה יְיָ אֱלֹהֵינוּ מֶלֶךְ הָעוֹלָם, אֲשֶׁר קִדְּשָׁנוּ בְּמִצְוֹתָיו, וְצִוָּנוּ
עַל בִּעוּר חָמֵץ.

Barukh atah Adonai Eloheinu Melech Ha-Olam, asher kid'shanu b'mitsvotav, v'tsivanu al bi-ur ḥameits.

Blessed are you, Lord our God, King of the Universe, who has sanctified us with His commandments, and commanded us to remove leaven.

(After the search is completed and the ḥameits is found, the following statement is made)

כָּל־חֲמִירָא וַחֲמִיעָא דְּאִכָּא בִרְשׁוּתִי דְּלָא חֲמִתֵּהּ וּדְלָא בִעַרְתֵּהּ
לִבְטִיל וְלֶהֱוֵי כְּעַפְרָא דְאַרְעָא.

Khal ḥamira va-ḥami-a d'ikha vir'shuti d'la ḥa'miteih ud'la va-a'riteih liv'tiyl v'leh'heveiy kh'af'ra d'ar'a.

May all ḥameits in my possession which I have not seen or removed be as nothing and be considered as dust of the earth.

(On the morning of the 14th of Nisan, the collected ḥameits is traditionally taken to a local synagogue as a place of disposal and burned. This can also be done at one's home, provided the burning of the ḥameits is done safely)

Preparing the Passover Table

There is quite of lot of preparation required for the actual Passover Seder: the purchase and preparation of the meal, including the traditional food items listed below for the Seder itself; wine and/or grape juice for those attending to drink four ceremonial cups during the Seder; a **Matsah-Tosh** (special pouch or plate to hold three pieces of matsah) along with a cloth napkin or pouch to "hide" the afikoman when it is made; and a **Zeroa** (either the roasted shankbone of a lamb or a chicken leg bone). An extra place setting with a special cup also needs to be set for Elijah the Prophet, just in case he shows up!

The following food items below are required and will be eaten as directed in this Haggadah during the Seder. These can be either on a traditional Seder Plate, or served out of simple plates and bowls.

- **Matsah:** enough for motsi, maror and ḥaroset - *unleavened bread, a reminder of the speed of G-d's redemption from Egypt*
- **Karpas:** celery, parsley or lettuce - *a reminder of life and prosperity*
- **Maror:** ground horseradish, either red or white - *a remembrance of the bitterness of our slavery in Egypt*
- **Ḥazeret:** romaine lettuce or slices of horseradish root - *a remembrance of the bitterness of our slavery in Egypt*
- **Ḥaroset:** mixture of chopped apples, nuts, honey, spices, wine or grape juice - *in remembrance of the mud bricks we were forced to make in Egypt as slaves*
- **Ḥagigah/Beitzah:** whole roasted hard-boiled egg with the shell on, displayed on the Seder Plate; shelled and quartered hard-boiled eggs in bowls to eat - *a reminder of the loss of the Ḥagigah (Festival sacrifice) eaten in Temple days*
- **Salt Water:** should look cloudy after it has been stirred up - *a representation of our sorrowfulness and tears as slaves in Egypt*

Candle Lighting

(Candles are traditionally lit before sundown on the first night of Passover by the women of the home reciting the following blessing; add words in parenthesis on Erev Shabbat)

בָּרוּךְ אַתָּה יְיָ אֱלֹהֵינוּ מֶלֶךְ הָעוֹלָם, אֲשֶׁר קִדְּשָׁנוּ בְּמִצְוֹתָיו, וְצִוָּנוּ
לְהַדְלִיק נֵר שֶׁל (שַׁבָּת וְשֶׁל) יוֹם טוֹב.

Barukh atah Adonai Eloheinu Melech Ha-Olam, asher kid'shanu b'mitsvotav, v'tsivanu l'hadlik neir shel (Shabbat v'shel) Yom Tov.

Blessed are you, Lord our God, King of the Universe, who has sanctified us with His commandments, and commanded us to light the (Shabbat and) Holiday lights.

בָּרוּךְ אַתָּה יְיָ אֱלֹהֵינוּ מֶלֶךְ הָעוֹלָם, אֲשֶׁר קִדְּשָׁנוּ בִּדְבָרוֹ, וְנָתַן לָנוּ
אֶת יֵשׁוּעַ מְשִׁיחֵנוּ, וְצִוָּנוּ לִהְיוֹת אוֹר לָעוֹלָם.

Barukh atah Adonai Eloheinu Melekh Ha'Olam, asher kid'shanu bidvaro, v'natan lanu et Yeishua Meshiḥeinu, v'tsivanu l'hiyot or la'olam.

Blessed are You, Lord our God, King of the Universe, who has sanctified us with his word, and has given us Yeshua our Messiah, and commanded us to be light to the world.

The Kiddush - the Cup of Sanctification:

The Kiddush, or sanctification, is the act of setting something apart for a holy purpose. In this case the something is a day: Passover. Occasionally Passover will begin on Friday evening, and as such both the celebration of Passover and the Shabbat must be set apart. To do so, there is a Kiddush unique to each that is recited at the beginning of the Passover Seder. However, if Passover begins on Saturday, or on any other day of the week, only the Kiddush for the Passover is recited.

Included in the Kiddush is the blessing over the first cup of wine to be drunk during the Passover Seder. A total of four specific cups are drunk, which have their meaning given from the text of Exodus 6:6-8 representing the four expressions of deliverance promised by God: "I will bring out," "I will deliver," "I will redeem," and "I will take."

This first cup is called, naturally enough, the Cup of Sanctification. Its name comes from the statement in Exodus 6:6, where God declared that He would bring us "out from the bondage of the Egyptians." This bringing out, or separation, from that which bound us to the Egyptians is exactly what the concept of the Kiddush means.

קַדֵּשׁ

(On Friday night begin here - Lift the First Cup and say)

(Quietly: וַיְהִי עֶרֶב וַיְהִי בֹקֶר) יוֹם הַשִּׁשִּׁי. וַיְכֻלּוּ הַשָּׁמַיִם וְהָאָרֶץ וְכָל
צְבָאָם. וַיְכַל אֱלֹהִים בַּיּוֹם הַשְּׁבִיעִי מְלַאכְתּוֹ אֲשֶׁר עָשָׂה, וַיִּשְׁבֹּת
בַּיּוֹם הַשְּׁבִיעִי מִכָּל מְלַאכְתּוֹ אֲשֶׁר עָשָׂה. וַיְבָרֶךְ אֱלֹהִים אֶת יוֹם
הַשְּׁבִיעִי וַיְקַדֵּשׁ אֹתוֹ, כִּי בוֹ שָׁבַת מִכָּל מְלַאכְתּוֹ אֲשֶׁר בָּרָא
אֱלֹהִים לַעֲשׂוֹת.

(Quietly: *Vay'hi erev vay'hi voker) yom hashishi. Vay'khulu hashamayim v'ha'arets v'khol ts'vaam. Vay'khal Elohim bayom hashvi'i m'lakhto asher asah, va'yishbot bayom hashvi'i mikol melakhto asher asah. Vayevarekh Elohim et yom hashvi'i vay'kadeish otoh, ki vo shavat mikol melakh'to asher barah Elohim la'asot.*

(On all other nights of the week begin here. On Shabbat add the words in parentheses)

בָּרוּךְ אַתָּה יְיָ אֱלֹהֵינוּ מֶלֶךְ הָעוֹלָם, בּוֹרֵא פְּרִי הַגָּפֶן.

Barukh atah Adonai Eloheinu Melekh Ha'Olam, borei p'ri ha'gafen.

בָּרוּךְ אַתָּה יְיָ אֱלֹהֵינוּ מֶלֶךְ הָעוֹלָם, אֲשֶׁר בָּחַר בָּנוּ מִכָּל עָם
וְרוֹמְמָנוּ מִכָּל לָשׁוֹן, וְקִדְּשָׁנוּ בְּמִצְוֹתָיו. וַתִּתֶּן לָנוּ יְיָ אֱלֹהֵינוּ
בְּאַהֲבָה (שַׁבָּתוֹת לִמְנוּחָה וּ) מוֹעֲדִים לְשִׂמְחָה, חַגִּים וּזְמַנִּים
לְשָׂשׂוֹן, אֶת יוֹם (הַשַּׁבָּת הַזֶּה וְאֶת יוֹם) חַג הַמַּצּוֹת הַזֶּה, זְמַן
חֵרוּתֵנוּ, (בְּאַהֲבָה) מִקְרָא קֹדֶשׁ, זֵכֶר לִיצִיאַת מִצְרָיִם. כִּי בָנוּ
בָחַרְתָּ וְאוֹתָנוּ קִדַּשְׁתָּ מִכָּל הָעַמִּים, (וְשַׁבָּת) וּמוֹעֲדֵי קָדְשֶׁךָ
(בְּאַהֲבָה וּבְרָצוֹן) בְּשִׂמְחָה וּבְשָׂשׂוֹן הִנְחַלְתָּנוּ.
בָּרוּךְ אַתָּה יְיָ, מְקַדֵּשׁ (הַשַּׁבָּת וְ) יִשְׂרָאֵל וְהַזְּמַנִּים.

Barukh atah Adonai Eloheinu Melekh Ha'Olam, asher baḥar banu mikol am v'rom'manu mikol lasot, v'kidshanu b'mitsvotayv. Vatiten lanu Adonai Eloheinu b'ahava (shabbatot lim'nuḥah u) moadim l'simḥah, ḥagim u-z'manim l'sason, et yom (haShabbat hazeh v'et yom) Ḥag HaMatsot hazeh, zeman ḥeiruteinu, (b'ahavah) mik'ra kodesh, zeikher litsiyat Mitsrayim. Ki vanu vaḥar'tah v'otanu kidash'ta mikol ha'amim, (v'Shabbat) u'moadei kad'shekha (b'ahavah uv'ratson) b'simḥah u'besason hin'ḥaltanu. Barukh atah Adonai, m'kadeish (haShabbat v') Yisraeil v'hazemanim.

Kadesh

(On Friday night begin here - Lift the First Cup and say)

(Quietly: And there was evening and there was morning) the sixth day. And thus the heavens, and the earth, and all their hosts were finished. And on the seventh day God completed all the work in which He had been engaged, and on the seventh day He rested from all the work which He had made. And God blessed the seventh day calling it holy, for on it He rested from all of the work which He had created.

(On all other nights of the week begin here. On Shabbat add the words in parentheses)

Blessed are You, Lord our God, King of the Universe, who creates the fruit of the vine.

Blessed are You, Lord our God, King of the Universe, who has chosen and exalted us above all nations, and has set us apart with your commandments. And You, Lord our God, have given us ***(Shabbats for rest,)*** holidays for gladness and festival seasons for joy, ***(this Shabbat day and)*** this day of the Festival of Matsah, our Festival of Freedom, ***(in love,)*** a holy assembly in remembrance of the exodus from Egypt. Surely You have chosen and set us apart from all other peoples, ***(and Shabbat),*** and the holy Festivals ***(in love and in favor)*** You have given us in happiness and joy. Blessed are You, Lord, who makes holy ***(the Shabbat,)*** Israel and the Festivals.

הבדלה

(On Saturday night, add the following)

בָּרוּךְ אַתָּה יְיָ, אֱלֹהֵינוּ מֶלֶךְ הָעוֹלָם, בּוֹרֵא מְאוֹרֵי הָאֵשׁ.

Barukh atah Adonai Eloheinu Melekh Ha'Olam, borei me'orei ha'eish.

בָּרוּךְ אַתָּה יְיָ, אֱלֹהֵינוּ מֶלֶךְ הָעוֹלָם, הַמַּבְדִּיל בֵּין קֹדֶשׁ לְחוֹל, בֵּין אוֹר לְחֹשֶׁךְ, בֵּין יִשְׂרָאֵל לָעַמִּים, בֵּין יוֹם הַשְּׁבִיעִי, לְשֵׁשֶׁת יְמֵי הַמַּעֲשֶׂה. בֵּין קְדֻשַּׁת שַׁבָּת לִקְדֻשַּׁת יוֹם טוֹב הִבְדַּלְתָּ. וְאֶת-יוֹם הַשְּׁבִיעִי מִשֵּׁשֶׁת יְמֵי הַמַּעֲשֶׂה קִדַּשְׁתָּ. הִבְדַּלְתָּ וְקִדַּשְׁתָּ אֶת-עַמְּךָ יִשְׂרָאֵל בִּקְדֻשָּׁתֶךָ. בָּרוּךְ אַתָּה יְיָ, הַמַּבְדִּיל בֵּין קֹדֶשׁ לְקֹדֶשׁ.

Barukh atah Adonai Eloheinu Melekh Ha'Olam, hamav'dil bein kodesh l'ḥol, bein ohr l'ḥoshekh, bein Yisraeil la'amim, bein yom hashvi'i, l'sheishet y'mei hama'aseh. Bein k'dushat Shabbat lik'dushat yom tov hiv'dalta. V'et yom hash'vi-i mi'sheishet y'mei hama'aseh kidash'ta. Hiv'dal'ta v'kidash'ta et am'kha Yisraeil bik'dushatekha. Barukh atah Adonai, hamav'dil bein kodesh l'kodesh.

(On the first night of Passover recite the Sheheḥeyanu blessing)

בָּרוּךְ אַתָּה יְיָ אֱלֹהֵינוּ מֶלֶךְ הָעוֹלָם, שֶׁהֶחֱיָנוּ, וְקִיְּמָנוּ, וְהִגִּיעָנוּ, לַזְּמַן הַזֶּה.

Barukh atah Adonai Eloheinu Melekh Ha'Olam, sheheḥeyanu, vekiyemanu, vehigiyanu, lazman hazeh!

(Drink the First Cup while reclining to the left)

ורחץ

(Wash your hands without saying a blessing)

כרפס

(The Leader of the Seder takes pieces of the karpas, dips it into salt water and distributes a piece to each person at the table. The karpas represents life, and is dipped into salt water which represents the sorrows of life. The following blessing is recited before eating)

בָּרוּךְ אַתָּה יְיָ, אֱלֹהֵינוּ מֶלֶךְ הָעוֹלָם, בּוֹרֵא פְּרִי הָאֲדָמָה.

Barukh atah Adonai, Eloheinu Melekh Ha'Olam, borei pri ha'adamah.

Havdalah

(On Saturday night, add the following)

Blessed are You, Lord our God, King of the Universe, who creates the light of the fire.

Blessed are You, Lord our God, for You have made a distinction between that which is holy and that which is common; between light and darkness; between Israel and the other nations; between the seventh day and the six days of work; between the sanctity of the Shabbat and the sanctity of the Festivals, distinguishing the sanctity of the seventh day from the six days of labor. You have set apart Israel Your people with Your holiness. Blessed are You, Lord, who has made a distinction between the holy and the profane.

(On the first night of Passover recite the Sheheḥeyanu blessing)

Blessed are You, Lord our God, King of the Universe, who has kept us, and sustained us, and enabled us to reach this season!

(Drink the First Cup while reclining to the left)

Urḥatz

(Wash your hands without saying a blessing)

Karpas

(The Leader of the Seder takes pieces of the karpas, dips it into salt water and distributes a piece to each person at the table. The karpas represents life, and is dipped into salt water which represents the sorrows of life. The following blessing is recited before eating)

Blessed are You, Lord our God, King of the Universe, who creates the fruit of the earth.

It is quite probable that it was at this very early part of the Passover Seder where Messiah Yeshua washed the feet of his Talmidim (disciples), as recorded in John 13.

יחץ

(The Leader of the Seder removes the middle matsah from the Matsah Tosh, breaking it in two. The smaller piece is returned to the Matsah Tosh and the larger piece is wrapped up in a white cloth as the Afikoman for after the meal)

מגיד

(The Leader of the Seder lifts the Seder Plate and the Matsah Tosh exposing the matsah for all to see. The telling of the Passover story begins with the following words)

הָא לַחְמָא עַנְיָא דִּי אֲכָלוּ אַבְהָתָנָא בְּאַרְעָא דְמִצְרָיִם.

Ha laḥma anya, di akha-lu av'hatana b'ar'a d'mitsra-yim!

כָּל דִּכְפִין יֵיתֵי וְיֵיכוֹל, כָּל דִּצְרִיךְ יֵיתֵי וְיִפְסַח. הָשַׁתָּא הָכָא, לְשָׁנָה הַבָּאָה בְּאַרְעָא דְיִשְׂרָאֵל. הָשַׁתָּא עַבְדֵי, לְשָׁנָה הַבָּאָה בְּנֵי חוֹרִין.

(The Seder Plate and Matsah Tosh are returned to the table and the Second Cup is filled)

(The youngest person at the table, who is able to read, asks the following four questions)

מַה נִּשְׁתַּנָּה הַלַּיְלָה הַזֶּה מִכָּל הַלֵּילוֹת?

Mah nish'tanah ha'lay'lah hazeh mikal ha-leilot?

שֶׁבְּכָל הַלֵּילוֹת אָנוּ אוֹכְלִין חָמֵץ וּמַצָּה. הַלַּיְלָה הַזֶּה כֻּלּוֹ מַצָּה?

She-b'khal haleilot anu okh'lin ḥameits umatsah. Ha-lay'lah hazeh kulo matsah?

שֶׁבְּכָל הַלֵּילוֹת אָנוּ אוֹכְלִין שְׁאָר יְרָקוֹת הַלַּיְלָה הַזֶּה מָרוֹר?

She-b'khal haleilot anu okh'lin sh'ar y'rakot Ha-lay'lah hazeh maror?

שֶׁבְּכָל הַלֵּילוֹת אֵין אָנוּ מַטְבִּילִין אֲפִילוּ פַּעַם אֶחָת. הַלַּיְלָה הַזֶּה שְׁתֵּי פְעָמִים?

She-b'khal haleiloht ein anu mat'bilin afilu pa-am eḥat. Ha-lay'lah hazeh sh'tei f'amim?

שֶׁבְּכָל הַלֵּילוֹת אָנוּ אוֹכְלִין בֵּין יוֹשְׁבִין וּבֵין מְסֻבִּין. הַלַּיְלָה הַזֶּה כֻּלָּנוּ מְסֻבִּין?

She-b'khal haleiloht anu okh'lin bein yosh'vin u-vein m'subin. Ha-lay'lah hazeh kulanu m'subin?

Yaḥats

(The Leader of the Seder removes the middle matsah from the Matsah Tosh, breaking it in two. The smaller piece is returned to the Matsah Tosh and the larger piece is wrapped up in a white cloth as the Afikoman for after the meal)

Maggid

(The Leader of the Seder lifts the Seder Plate and the Matsah Tosh exposing the matsah for all to see. The telling of the Passover story begins with the following words)

Our fathers ate this bread of affliction in the land of Egypt.

You who are hungry come and eat. You who are needy, come and celebrate the Passover with us. At present we are here, next year may we be in the land of Israel. Now we are like slaves, next year may we be like free people.

(The Seder Plate and Matsah Tosh are returned to the table and the Second Cup is filled)

(The youngest person at the table, who is able to read, asks the following four questions)

Why is this night different from all other nights?

On all other nights we may eat leavened bread or unleavened bread.
Why is it that on this night we may eat only unleavened bread?

On all other nights we may eat herbs of any kind.
Why is it that on this night we eat only bitter herbs?

On all other nights we don't have to dip our herbs even once.
Why is it that on this night we must dip them twice?

On all other nights we may eat our meal in any manner we choose.
Why is it that on this night we recline at the table together while we eat?

Why ask the Four Questions?

The Four Questions above developed in the Middle Ages out of three questions found in the Mishnah: why do we dip twice, why do we eat only matsah and why do we eat only roasted meat.

One of the things that is often missed in the celebration of the Passover Seder is the fact that this is not an "adult time." Rather, it is a time to engage the children in the telling of a story. As a result, there is a balance that is maintained between the formality of the service and the sheer pleasure of telling a story. The questions above aid us in setting the stage for the telling of the story. In fact, the whole story on the next page about our sages lost in the telling of the story is a reminder that even as adults we should take joy in the telling and retelling of a story such as this.

(Expose the matsah in the Matsah Tosh and begin telling the story)

עֲבָדִים הָיִינוּ לְפַרְעֹה בְּמִצְרָיִם. וַיּוֹצִיאֵנוּ יְיָ אֱלֹהֵינוּ מִשָּׁם, בְּיָד חֲזָקָה וּבִזְרוֹעַ נְטוּיָה, וְאִלּוּ לֹא הוֹצִיא הַקָּדוֹשׁ בָּרוּךְ הוּא אֶת־אֲבוֹתֵינוּ מִמִּצְרַיִם, הֲרֵי אָנוּ וּבָנֵינוּ וּבְנֵי בָנֵינוּ, מְשֻׁעְבָּדִים הָיִינוּ לְפַרְעֹה בְּמִצְרָיִם.

וַאֲפִילוּ כֻּלָּנוּ חֲכָמִים, כֻּלָּנוּ נְבוֹנִים, כֻּלָּנוּ זְקֵנִים, כֻּלָּנוּ יוֹדְעִים אֶת־הַתּוֹרָה, מִצְוָה עָלֵינוּ לְסַפֵּר בִּיצִיאַת מִצְרָיִם. וְכָל הַמַּרְבֶּה לְסַפֵּר בִּיצִיאַת מִצְרַיִם, הֲרֵי זֶה מְשֻׁבָּח.

מַעֲשֶׂה בְּרַבִּי אֱלִיעֶזֶר, וְרַבִּי יְהוֹשֻׁעַ, וְרַבִּי אֶלְעָזָר בֶּן־עֲזַרְיָה, וְרַבִּי עֲקִיבָא, וְרַבִּי טַרְפוֹן, שֶׁהָיוּ מְסֻבִּין בִּבְנֵי־בְרַק, וְהָיוּ מְסַפְּרִים בִּיצִיאַת מִצְרַיִם, כָּל־אוֹתוֹ הַלַּיְלָה, עַד שֶׁבָּאוּ תַלְמִידֵיהֶם וְאָמְרוּ לָהֶם: רַבּוֹתֵינוּ, הִגִּיעַ זְמַן קְרִיאַת שְׁמַע, שֶׁל שַׁחֲרִית.

אָמַר רַבִּי אֶלְעָזָר בֶּן־עֲזַרְיָה, הֲרֵי אֲנִי כְּבֶן שִׁבְעִים שָׁנָה, וְלֹא זָכִיתִי, שֶׁתֵּאָמֵר יְצִיאַת מִצְרַיִם בַּלֵּילוֹת, עַד שֶׁדְּרָשָׁהּ בֶּן זוֹמָא. שֶׁנֶּאֱמַר: לְמַעַן תִּזְכֹּר, אֶת יוֹם צֵאתְךָ מֵאֶרֶץ מִצְרַיִם, כֹּל יְמֵי חַיֶּיךָ. יְמֵי חַיֶּיךָ הַיָּמִים. כֹּל יְמֵי חַיֶּיךָ הַלֵּילוֹת. וַחֲכָמִים אוֹמְרִים: יְמֵי חַיֶּיךָ הָעוֹלָם הַזֶּה. כֹּל יְמֵי חַיֶּיךָ לְהָבִיא לִימוֹת הַמָּשִׁיחַ.

(Expose the matsah in the Matsah Tosh and begin telling the story)

Once, long ago, our fathers were slaves of Pharaoh in Egypt, when the Lord our God redeemed us and brought us out of Egypt by the power of His hand and the glory of His outstretched arm. Had not the Holy One, blessed is He, brought our fathers out of Egypt, then we, our children and our children's children would still be slaves in Egypt.

Therefore, even if we were wise and learned in all things; even if we were old and learned in the teachings of Torah, it would still be our duty to tell the story of our deliverance from slavery. In fact, the more we tell this story of our redemption the more He is to be praised.

It is said that Rabbi Eliezer, Rabbi Joshua, Rabbi Elazar ben Azariah, Rabbi Akiva and Rabbi Tarfon sat through the whole night, in the house of Berak telling the story of the exodus from Egypt. As dawn was approaching their students arrived to begin morning prayer. They were surprised when they saw their Rabbis were still engaged in the telling of the Passover story, and they called out to them, "Our teachers, it is time now to declare the Shema during shacharit."

When he realized what time it was, Rabbi Elazar ben Azariah said, "I am seventy years old and I still didn't understand why the story of the coming out of Egypt is to be told at night, until ben Zoma explained it. We are told that we are to remember the day of our going out from Egypt all the days of our life. He said, 'The days of your life could be understood to mean only the days; however, all the days of your life includes the nights as well.' Another explanation is this: 'The days of your life' refers to this world only, but 'all the days of your life' includes the time of Messiah as well."

ארבעה בנים

Leader : בָּרוּךְ הַמָּקוֹם. בָּרוּךְ הוּא. בָּרוּךְ שֶׁנָּתַן תּוֹרָה לְעַמּוֹ יִשְׂרָאֵל. בָּרוּךְ הוּא כְּנֶגֶד אַרְבָּעָה בָנִים דִּבְּרָה תוֹרָה. אֶחָד חָכָם, וְאֶחָד רָשָׁע, וְאֶחָד תָּם, וְאֶחָד שֶׁאֵינוֹ יוֹדֵעַ לִשְׁאוֹל.

All : חָכָם מַה הוּא אוֹמֵר, מָה הָעֵדֹת וְהַחֻקִּים וְהַמִּשְׁפָּטִים, אֲשֶׁר צִוָּה יְיָ אֱלֹהֵינוּ אֶתְכֶם?

Leader : וְאַף אַתָּה אֱמָר־לוֹ כְּהִלְכוֹת הַפֶּסַח אֵין מַפְטִירִין אַחַר הַפֶּסַח אֲפִיקוֹמָן.

All : רָשָׁע מַה הוּא אוֹמֵר, מָה הָעֲבֹדָה הַזֹּאת לָכֶם?

Leader : לָכֶם וְלֹא לוֹ. וּלְפִי שֶׁהוֹצִיא אֶת־עַצְמוֹ מִן הַכְּלָל, כָּפַר בָּעִקָּר. וְאַף אַתָּה הַקְהֵה אֶת־שִׁנָּיו, וֶאֱמָר־לוֹ. בַּעֲבוּר זֶה, עָשָׂה יְיָ לִי, בְּצֵאתִי מִמִּצְרָיִם, לִי וְלֹא־לוֹ. אִלּוּ הָיָה שָׁם, לֹא הָיָה נִגְאָל.

All : תָּם מַה הוּא אוֹמֵר, מַה זֹּאת?

Leader : וְאָמַרְתָּ אֵלָיו: בְּחֹזֶק יָד הוֹצִיאָנוּ יְיָ מִמִּצְרַיִם, מִבֵּית עֲבָדִים.

All : וְשֶׁאֵינוֹ יוֹדֵעַ לִשְׁאוֹל, אַתְּ פְּתַח לוֹ, שֶׁנֶּאֱמַר.

Leader : וְהִגַּדְתָּ לְבִנְךָ בַּיּוֹם הַהוּא לֵאמֹר, בַּעֲבוּר זֶה עָשָׂה יְיָ לִי בְּצֵאתִי מִמִּצְרָיִם.

(Raise your cup and recite)

וְהִיא שֶׁעָמְדָה לַאֲבוֹתֵינוּ וְלָנוּ. שֶׁלֹּא אֶחָד בִּלְבָד עָמַד עָלֵינוּ לְכַלּוֹתֵנוּ, אֶלָּא שֶׁבְּכָל דּוֹר וָדוֹר עוֹמְדִים עָלֵינוּ לְכַלּוֹתֵנוּ, וְהַקָּדוֹשׁ בָּרוּךְ הוּא מַצִּילֵנוּ מִיָּדָם.

(Put your cup down without drinking from it)

The Four Sons

Leader: Blessed is the All Present One; blessed is He. Blessed is the Giver of Torah to the people of Israel; blessed is He. The Torah tells us of four sons; a son who is wise, a son who is wicked, a son who is honest, and a son who is too young to know what questions to ask.

All: The son who is wise asks, "What is the meaning of the rules, laws and customs the Lord our God has given us?"

Leader: You shall explain to him the meaning of all of the laws of the Passover, including that there is no eating of Afikoman after the Passover Lamb.

All: The son who is wicked asks, "What is the meaning of this service to you?"

Leader: By saying, "you" he excludes himself from the community; he denies a basic principle. Therefore, you shall tell him clearly: "I am doing this service because of what the Lord did for me when I came forth from the land of Egypt." It is for me and not for him. Indeed, if he had been there, he would not have been redeemed.

All: The son who is honest simply asks, "What is this?"

Leader: You shall answer him by saying, "With strength of hand the Lord took us out of the land of Egypt; out of slavery."

All: As to the son who does not know what question he should ask, what should we say to him?

Leader: You shall tell your child in that day, "This is done because of what the Lord did for me when I came forth from the land of Egypt."

(Raise your cup and recite)

And this promise has been for our ancestors and us. For not only just one enemy has risen against us to destroy us, but in every generation there are those who rise up against us to destroy us, but the Holy One, blessed be He, saves us from their hand.

(Put your cup down without drinking from it)

(Tell or read the story of the Passover as if to the youngest child. Traditionally, the name of Moses is mentioned only once and alluded to only once in the Haggadah. We've included his name here because without Moses, there would be no story)

A long time ago our ancestors worshiped idols. One day, God visited a man named Abram, the father of our people, and told him to leave his home and his family. Abram was to travel to a new land that God would give to him and his children forever. God changed Abram's name to Abraham, and warned him that his descendants would become slaves, but after four hundred years God would redeem them. Abraham obeyed God and promised that he and his family would love and serve only the One True God, the Creator of Heaven and Earth. Some time later, Abraham and his wife Sarah had a son named Isaac. Isaac obeyed his parents and lived as Abraham had taught him, and when he grew up he married Rivkah. Isaac and Rivkah had two sons, Jacob and Esau. The older brother, Esau, did whatever he saw his neighbors doing; but Jacob decided to walk in the ways of God, following his father Isaac and his grandfather Abraham. Jacob married Leah and Rachel, and between his wives and their handmaids, Bilhah and Zilpah, Jacob had twelve sons and one daughter. God gave Jacob a new name, which was Israel; after that, his family was known as "the Sons of Israel" or the Israelites.

One day, Rachel's oldest son Joseph was sold into slavery by his jealous brothers. They lied to their father Jacob, telling him that Joseph had been killed by a wild animal, which made Jacob very sad. Joseph became a slave to an important man in the land of Egypt. He had many adventures while in Egypt, and God was with him through it all. One night, God sent Pharaoh a dream, then helped Joseph tell Pharaoh that the dream was about the future. Because of this, Pharaoh made Joseph second in command over all Egypt. Joseph eventually reunited with his father and his brothers, and he brought all of them with their families to Egypt to live in a place called Goshen. This was a time of peace and goodness, and our people multiplied. Soon the land was filled with Jacob's huge family, and they were given another name – the Hebrews.

After a while, Jacob and Joseph died, and a new Pharaoh ruled in Egypt. This Pharaoh became afraid of the growing number of Israelites. There were so many people in Jacob's family that he worried they would side with his enemies and defeat him, so Pharaoh decided to make them all his slaves. The Israelites were forced to work hard gathering straw from the fields and making bricks to build cities. Our people suffered in this way for many years. But the more they suffered, the greater the number of Israelites grew. To stop this, Pharaoh told the Egyptians to kill all the Hebrew boys.

At this time, one Hebrew woman gave birth to a baby boy. She and her husband hid him in their home, but as he grew it became harder to do so. Finally, they could not hide their son anymore. They placed him in a reed basket on the River Nile, hoping that God would save his life. And that is exactly what God did! Just at the time when Pharaoh's daughter was bathing in the Nile, the basket carrying the Hebrew boy drifted by. Pharaoh's daughter sent her servants to bring her the basket, and when she saw the baby she immediately fell in love with him. She adopted him as her son, named him Moses, and raised him in Pharaoh's house.

Moses grew up as a Prince in Egypt, but he never could forget that he was really a Hebrew, just like the slaves in the field. One day he saw an Egyptian soldier beating a Hebrew slave and when he thought no one was looking, he killed the Egyptian and buried him in the sand. However, a few days later it became clear that other people knew, and Moses ran for his life from Pharaoh. He crossed the desert and ended up in a place called Midian. There, Moses met his wife, Zipporah, and for forty years he took care of his father-in-law's sheep. After all this time he saw an amazing sight. Up in the hills, Moses saw a bush that seemed to be burning, but didn't burn up. Thinking that this was very odd, Moses decided to go and see. He climbed the mountain to the spot where the burning bush was and he heard a voice who said to him, "I am the Lord, the God of Abraham, Isaac, and Jacob. I have heard the cries of my people and it is time that they be set free. Moses, I have chosen you to go to Pharaoh and tell him for Me to let My people Israel go, so they will worship Me." Well, Moses was surprised and troubled. He didn't want to go back to Egypt. He tried to talk God out of sending him to speak to Pharaoh, but Moses lost the argument and in the end he returned to Egypt to give Pharaoh God's message.

No matter how many times, or in how many ways Moses asked Pharaoh to let the Israelis go, Pharaoh wouldn't listen. After all, if he let them go who would be his slaves? Who would build his cities? It seemed that the only word Pharaoh knew was "NO!" He said, "I don't know your God! Why should I listen to Him? I will not let your people go!" God is patient, but he expects to be obeyed. Moses soon said to Pharaoh, "If you don't let My people go I will send plagues on you and all of the land of Egypt. In fact I will continue to send plague after plague until you know that I am God and agree to let My people go!"

Leader : **וַיּוֹצִאֵנוּ יְיָ מִמִּצְרַיִם בְּיָד חֲזָקָה, וּבִזְרֹעַ נְטוּיָה, וּבְמֹרָא גָּדֹל, וּבְאֹתוֹת וּבְמֹפְתִים.**

All : **וַיּוֹצִאֵנוּ יְיָ מִמִּצְרַיִם. לֹא עַל יְדֵי מַלְאָךְ, וְלֹא עַל יְדֵי שָׂרָף, וְלֹא עַל יְדֵי שָׁלִיחַ, אֶלָּא הַקָּדוֹשׁ בָּרוּךְ הוּא בִּכְבוֹדוֹ וּבְעַצְמוֹ. שֶׁנֶּאֱמַר: וְעָבַרְתִּי בְאֶרֶץ מִצְרַיִם בַּלַּיְלָה הַזֶּה, וְהִכֵּיתִי כָל־בְּכוֹר בְּאֶרֶץ מִצְרַיִם מֵאָדָם וְעַד בְּהֵמָה, וּבְכָל אֱלֹהֵי מִצְרַיִם אֶעֱשֶׂה שְׁפָטִים. אֲנִי יְיָ.**

Leader : **וְעָבַרְתִּי בְאֶרֶץ מִצְרַיִם בַּלַּיְלָה הַזֶּה, אֲנִי וְלֹא מַלְאָךְ. וְהִכֵּיתִי כָל בְּכוֹר בְּאֶרֶץ־מִצְרַיִם, אֲנִי וְלֹא שָׂרָף. וּבְכָל־אֱלֹהֵי מִצְרַיִם אֶעֱשֶׂה שְׁפָטִים, אֲנִי וְלֹא הַשָּׁלִיחַ. אֲנִי יְיָ. אֲנִי הוּא וְלֹא אַחֵר.**

All : **בְּיָד חֲזָקָה, זוֹ הַדֶּבֶר, כְּמָה שֶׁנֶּאֱמַר: הִנֵּה יַד יְיָ הוֹיָה בְּמִקְנְךָ אֲשֶׁר בַּשָּׂדֶה, בַּסּוּסִים, בַּחֲמֹרִים, בַּגְּמַלִּים, בַּבָּקָר וּבַצֹּאן, דֶּבֶר כָּבֵד מְאֹד.**

Leader : **וּבִזְרֹעַ נְטוּיָה, זוֹ הַחֶרֶב, כְּמָה שֶׁנֶּאֱמַר: וְחַרְבּוֹ שְׁלוּפָה בְּיָדוֹ, נְטוּיָה עַל יְרוּשָׁלָיִם.**

All : **וּבְמוֹרָא גָּדֹל, זוֹ גִּלּוּי שְׁכִינָה. כְּמָה שֶׁנֶּאֱמַר: אוֹ הֲנִסָּה אֱלֹהִים לָבוֹא לָקַחַת לוֹ גוֹי מִקֶּרֶב גּוֹי בְּמַסֹּת בְּאֹתֹת וּבְמוֹפְתִים וּבְמִלְחָמָה וּבְיָד חֲזָקָה וּבִזְרוֹעַ נְטוּיָה וּבְמוֹרָאִים גְּדוֹלִים כְּכֹל אֲשֶׁר־עָשָׂה לָכֶם יְיָ אֱלֹהֵיכֶם בְּמִצְרַיִם לְעֵינֶיךָ.**

Leader : **וּבְאֹתוֹת, זֶה הַמַּטֶּה, כְּמָה שֶׁנֶּאֱמַר: וְאֶת הַמַּטֶּה הַזֶּה תִּקַּח בְּיָדֶךָ, אֲשֶׁר תַּעֲשֶׂה בּוֹ אֶת הָאֹתוֹת.**

All : **וּבְמֹפְתִים, זֶה הַדָּם, כְּמָה שֶׁנֶּאֱמַר: וְנָתַתִּי מוֹפְתִים בַּשָּׁמַיִם וּבָאָרֶץ.**

Leader : **אֵלּוּ עֶשֶׂר מַכּוֹת שֶׁהֵבִיא הַקָּדוֹשׁ, בָּרוּךְ הוּא, עַל־הַמִּצְרִים בְּמִצְרַיִם, וְאֵלּוּ הֵן: דָּם, צְפַרְדֵּעַ, כִּנִּים, עָרוֹב, דֶּבֶר, שְׁחִין, בָּרָד, אַרְבֶּה, חֹשֶׁךְ, מַכַּת בְּכוֹרוֹת.**

Leader: And the Lord took us out of Egypt with a strong hand and with an outstretched arm and with great awe and with signs and with wonders.

All: **And the Lord took us out of Egypt. Not through an angel and not through a seraph and not through a messenger, but personally the Holy One, blessed be He, Himself. As it says, "And I will pass through the Land of Egypt on that night and I will smite every firstborn in the Land of Egypt, from men to animals; and with all the gods of Egypt, I will make judgments. I am the Lord."**

Leader: "And I will pass through the Land of Egypt this night, I and not an angel. And I will smite every firstborn, I and not a seraph. And with all the gods of Egypt, I will make judgments, I and not a messenger. I am the Lord. I am He and there is no other."

All: **With a strong hand, refers to the pestilence, as it says, "Behold the hand of the Lord is upon your herds that are in the field, upon the horses, upon the donkeys, upon the camels, upon the cattle and upon the flocks, they will suffer a very heavy pestilence."**

Leader: And with an outstretched forearm, this refers to the sword, as it says, "And his sword was drawn in his hand, leaning over Jerusalem."

All: **And with great awe, this refers to the revelation of the Divine Presence, as it says, "Or has any god ever tried to take for Himself a nation from within a nation with trials, with signs and with wonders and with war and with a strong hand and with an outstretched arm and with great and awesome acts, like all that the Lord, your God, did for you in Egypt in front of your eyes?"**

Leader: And with signs, refers to the staff, as it says, "And this staff you shall take in your hand, that with it you will perform signs."

All: **And with wonders, refers to blood, as it says, "And I will place my wonders in the skies and in the earth."**

Leader: These are the plagues that the Holy One, blessed be He, brought on the Egyptians in Egypt: **Blood, Frogs, Lice, Flies, Livestock Disease, Boils, Hail, Locusts, Darkness, Death of the Firstborn.**

(After speaking about each plague, pronounce it loudly in Hebrew then English, and instruct everyone at the table to remove a drop from their Second Cup for each plague and place the drop onto their plate)

All: And the Lord spoke to Moses, "Say to Aaron: Take your rod, and stretch out your hand upon the waters of Egypt, upon their streams, upon their rivers, and upon their ponds, and upon all their pools of water, that they may become blood; and that there may be blood throughout all the land of Egypt, both in utensils of wood, and in utensils of stone."

Leader:* דָּם *(Dahm) **Blood**

All: And the Lord spoke to Moses, "Say to Aaron: Stretch forth your hand with your rod over the streams, over the rivers, and over the ponds, and cause frogs to come up upon the land of Egypt."

Leader:* צְפַרְדֵּעַ *(Tz'fardei'a) **Frogs**

All: And the Lord said to Moses, "Say to Aaron, Stretch out your rod, and strike the dust of the land, that it may become lice throughout all the land of Egypt."

Leader:* כִּנִּים *(Kinim) **Lice**

All: And the Lord said to Moses, "Rise up early in the morning, and stand before Pharaoh when he comes to the water; and say to him: Thus says the Lord, 'Let My people go, that they may serve Me. If you will not let My people go, behold, I will send swarms of biting insects upon you, and upon your servants, and upon your people, and into your houses.'"

Leader:* עָרוֹב *(Arov) **Flies**

All: Then the Lord said to Moses, "Go to Pharaoh, and tell him, Thus says the Lord God of the Hebrews, 'Let My people go, that they may serve Me. If you refuse to let them go, and continue to hold them, behold, the hand of the Lord will be against your cattle in the field, the horses, the donkeys, the camels... there will be a very great plague.'"

Leader:* דֶּבֶר *(Dever) **Livestock Disease**

All: And the Lord said to Moses and to Aaron, "Take handfuls of ashes from the furnace, and let Moses sprinkle it toward the heavens in the sight of Pharaoh. And it shall become fine dust in all the land of Egypt, and boils shall break out with sores upon man, and upon beast, throughout all the land of Egypt."

Leader:* שְׁחִין *(Sh'ḥin) **Boils**

All: And the Lord said to Moses, "Stretch out your hand toward the heavens, that there may be hail in all the land of Egypt, upon man, and upon beast, and upon every herb of the field, throughout the land of Egypt."

Leader:* בָּרָד *(Bah'rad) **Hail**

All: And the Lord said to Moses, "Stretch out your hand over the land of Egypt for the locusts, that they may come upon the land of Egypt, and eat every herb of the land, all that the hail has left."

Leader:* אַרְבֶּה *(Ar'beh) **Locusts**

All: And the Lord said to Moses, "Stretch out your hand toward the heavens, that there may be darkness over the land of Egypt, darkness which may be felt." And Moses stretched out his hand toward heaven; and there was a thick darkness in all the land of Egypt for three days; no one could see anything, nor did anyone go out from his place for three days; but all the people of Israel had light in their dwellings.

Leader:* חֹשֶׁךְ *(Ḥoshekh) **Darkness**

All: And Moses said, "Thus says the Lord, 'About midnight will I go out into the midst of Egypt; and all the firstborn in the land of Egypt shall die, from the firstborn of Pharaoh who sits on his throne, even to the firstborn of the maidservant who is behind the mill; and all the firstborn of beasts. And there shall be a great cry throughout all the land of Egypt, such as there has never been, nor shall there be another like it again. But against any of the people of Israel shall not a dog move his tongue, against man or beast; that you may know that the Lord does put a difference between the Egyptians and Israel.' " And it came to pass, that at midnight the Lord struck all the firstborn in the land of Egypt, from the firstborn of Pharaoh who sat on his throne to the firstborn of the captive who was in the dungeon; and all the firstborn of cattle.

Leader: מַכַּת בְּכוֹרוֹת *(Makat b'khorot)* Death of the First Born

All: And Pharaoh rose up in the night, he, and all his servants, and all the Egyptians; and there was a great cry in Egypt; for there was not a house where there was not one dead. And he called for Moses and Aaron by night, and said, "Rise up, and get out from among my people, both you and the people of Israel; and go, serve the Lord, as you have said."

These are the Requirements of the Passover:

“This will be the first month of the year to you. On the tenth day of this month, every head of every household is to take a lamb, one lamb per house; and if the household is too small for a whole lamb, neighboring households can join together, as long as every person gets enough to eat. Your lamb must be strong and healthy, a male one year old; you will take it out from the sheep or from the goats; and you will keep your lamb until the fourteenth day of the same month; and everyone who belongs to the family of Israel will kill their lamb in the evening just before sunset.

“And they will take the lamb’s blood, and smear it on the two side posts and on the upper door post of the houses where they will eat it. And they will eat the meat roasted with fire on that night, and unleavened bread; and they will eat it with bitter herbs. You must roast the whole lamb with fire: you are not to cook it any other way, nor remove the head, legs, or innards. You will eat all the meat before morning; and anything left until the morning you will burn in the fire.

“This is the way you will eat it: with your clothes on, your shoes on your feet and your staff in your hand; and you will eat it in haste; it is the Lord’s Passover. For I will pass through the land of Egypt on this night, and will kill all the firstborn in the land of Egypt, both man and beast; and against all the gods of Egypt I will execute judgment; I am the Lord. And the blood will be a sign upon the houses where you are; and when I see the blood, I will pass over you, and you will not die when I strike the land of Egypt.

"And you will celebrate the Festival of Unleavened Bread, for on this same day I brought your armies out of the land of Egypt; therefore, you will celebrate this day by an unchanging law for all the generations to come. You will celebrate it as a festival to the Lord—a lasting command. In the first month, from the evening of the fourteenth day you are to eat unleavened bread until the evening of the twenty-first day. For seven days you are to eat unleavened bread, and no leaven is to be found in your houses. On the first day remove the leaven from your houses, for anyone, whether foreigner or native-born, who eats anything with leaven in it from the first day through the seventh will be cut off from the community of Israel. Wherever you live, you must eat unleavened bread. On the first day hold a sacred assembly, and another one on the seventh day. Do no work at all on these assembly days, except to prepare food you need to eat during these special days; that is all you may do.

"And you are required to celebrate this festival – you and your children forever. And it shall come to pass, when you come to the land which the Lord will give you, according to His promise, that you will keep this service. And when your children ask you, 'Why do we do this? What does it mean?' you will answer, 'It is the sacrifice of the Passover of the Lord, who passed over the houses of the people of Israel in Egypt, when He struck the Egyptians, and saved our people.'"

And the people bowed their heads and worshiped. And the people of Israel went away, and did just as the Lord had commanded Moses and Aaron.

כַּמָּה מַעֲלוֹת טוֹבוֹת לַמָּקוֹם עָלֵֽינוּ!

אִלּוּ הוֹצִיאָֽנוּ מִמִּצְרַֽיִם, וְלֹא עָשָׂה בָהֶם שְׁפָטִים, דַּיֵּֽנוּ!
אִלּוּ עָשָׂה בָהֶם שְׁפָטִים, וְלֹא עָשָׂה בֵאלֹהֵיהֶם, דַּיֵּֽנוּ!
אִלּוּ עָשָׂה בֵאלֹהֵיהֶם, וְלֹא הָרַג אֶת־בְּכוֹרֵיהֶם, דַּיֵּֽנוּ!
אִלּוּ הָרַג אֶת־בְּכוֹרֵיהֶם, וְלֹא נָֽתַן לָֽנוּ אֶת־מָמוֹנָם, דַּיֵּֽנוּ!
אִלּוּ נָֽתַן לָֽנוּ אֶת־מָמוֹנָם, וְלֹא קָֽרַע לָֽנוּ אֶת־הַיָּם, דַּיֵּֽנוּ!
אִלּוּ קָֽרַע לָֽנוּ אֶת־הַיָּם, וְלֹא הֶעֱבִירָֽנוּ בְתוֹכוֹ בֶּחָרָבָה, דַּיֵּֽנוּ!
אִלּוּ הֶעֱבִירָֽנוּ בְתוֹכוֹ בֶּחָרָבָה, וְלֹא שִׁקַּע צָרֵֽינוּ בְּתוֹכוֹ, דַּיֵּֽנוּ!
אִלּוּ שִׁקַּע צָרֵֽינוּ בְּתוֹכוֹ, וְלֹא סִפֵּק צָרְכֵּֽנוּ בַּמִּדְבָּר אַרְבָּעִים שָׁנָה, דַּיֵּֽנוּ!
אִלּוּ סִפֵּק צָרְכֵּֽנוּ בַּמִּדְבָּר אַרְבָּעִים שָׁנָה, וְלֹא הֶאֱכִילָֽנוּ אֶת־הַמָּן, דַּיֵּֽנוּ!
אִלּוּ הֶאֱכִילָֽנוּ אֶת־הַמָּן, וְלֹא נָֽתַן לָֽנוּ אֶת־הַשַּׁבָּת, דַּיֵּֽנוּ!
אִלּוּ נָֽתַן לָֽנוּ אֶת־הַשַּׁבָּת, וְלֹא קֵֽרְבָֽנוּ לִפְנֵי הַר סִינַי, דַּיֵּֽנוּ!
אִלּוּ קֵֽרְבָֽנוּ לִפְנֵי הַר סִינַי, וְלֹא נָֽתַן לָֽנוּ אֶת־הַתּוֹרָה, דַּיֵּֽנוּ!
אִלּוּ נָֽתַן לָֽנוּ אֶת־הַתּוֹרָה, וְלֹא הִכְנִיסָֽנוּ לְאֶֽרֶץ יִשְׂרָאֵל, דַּיֵּֽנוּ!
אִלּוּ הִכְנִיסָֽנוּ לְאֶֽרֶץ יִשְׂרָאֵל, וְלֹא בָֽנָה לָֽנוּ אֶת־בֵּית הַבְּחִירָה, דַּיֵּֽנוּ!

עַל אַחַת כַּמָּה וְכַמָּה טוֹבָה כְפוּלָה וּמְכֻפֶּֽלֶת לַמָּקוֹם עָלֵֽינוּ!

שֶׁהוֹצִיאָֽנוּ מִמִּצְרַֽיִם, וְעָשָׂה בָהֶם שְׁפָטִים, וְעָשָׂה בֵאלֹהֵיהֶם, וְהָרַג אֶת־בְּכוֹרֵיהֶם, וְנָֽתַן לָֽנוּ אֶת־מָמוֹנָם, וְקָֽרַע לָֽנוּ אֶת־הַיָּם, וְהֶעֱבִירָֽנוּ בְתוֹכוֹ בֶּחָרָבָה, וְשִׁקַּע צָרֵֽינוּ בְּתוֹכוֹ, וְסִפֵּק צָרְכֵּֽנוּ בַּמִּדְבָּר אַרְבָּעִים שָׁנָה, וְהֶאֱכִילָֽנוּ אֶת־הַמָּן, וְנָֽתַן לָֽנוּ אֶת־הַשַּׁבָּת, וְקֵֽרְבָֽנוּ לִפְנֵי הַר סִינַי, וְנָֽתַן לָֽנוּ אֶת־הַתּוֹרָה, וְהִכְנִיסָֽנוּ לְאֶֽרֶץ יִשְׂרָאֵל, וּבָֽנָה לָֽנוּ אֶת־בֵּית הַבְּחִירָה.

וְשָׁלַח לָֽנוּ אֶת־יֵשׁוּעַ מְשִׁיחֵֽנוּ בְּעֵת רְצוֹנוֹ!

Dayenu expresses the essence of thankfulness toward our God. Instead of always looking for more, it is a declaration that we are satisfied with whatever God chooses to give us. We can say ***"Dayenu: It would have been enough"***, because we know the nature of our God, and it is His nature not to withold any good thing from His children. As we look at this list of what He has done for us we could probably think of many other things to be thankful for. God not only gave us all the things listed above, but in the fullness of time He sent Messiah Yeshua, our Passover. If He had done nothing else we would say with great joy and without reservation: *"It would have been enough!"*

A transliterated version of a few verses of Dayenu is located on page 64 if you'd like to sing it!

How grateful we are for all the good that was done for us!

Had He only taken us out of Egypt, and not brought judgment on them: It would have been enough for us!

Had He only brought judgment on them, and not upon their gods: It would have been enough for us!

Had He only brought judgment upon their gods, and not slain their firstborn: It would have been enough for us!

Had He only slain their firstborn, and not given us their wealth: It would have been enough for us!

Had He only given us their wealth, and not divided the sea: It would have been enough for us!

Had He only divided the sea, and not brought us through on dry ground: It would have been enough for us!

Had He only brought us through on dry ground, and not drowned our oppressors: It would have been enough for us!

Had He only drowned our oppressors, and not met our needs in the wilderness: It would have been enough for us!

Had He only met our needs in the wilderness, and not fed us with manna: It would have been enough for us!

Had He only fed us with manna, and not given us the Shabbat: It would have been enough for us!

Had He only given us the Shabbat, and not brought us to Mount Sinai: It would have been enough for us!

Had He only brought us to Mount Sinai, and not given us the Torah: It would have been enough for us!

Had He only given us the Torah, and not brought us into the land of Israel: It would have been enough for us!

Had He only brought us into the land of Israel, and not built for us His Chosen House: It would have been enough for us!

How grateful we are then for all these acts of goodness, kindness, and mercy which were bestowed on us!

God brought us out of Egypt. He brought judgment upon them and upon their gods. He slew their firstborn. He gave us their wealth. He divided the Sea. He brought us through it on dry ground. He drowned our oppressors in it. He met all our needs in the wilderness. He fed us with manna. He gave us the Shabbat. He brought us to Mount Sinai. He gave us the Torah. He brought us into the land of Israel, and He built for us His Chosen House, the Temple.

And He sent Yeshua, our Messiah, at the time pleasing to Him!

רַבָּן גַּמְלִיאֵל הָיָה אוֹמֵר, כָּל שֶׁלֹּא אָמַר שְׁלֹשָׁה דְבָרִים אֵלּוּ בַּפֶּסַח, לֹא יָצָא יְדֵי חוֹבָתוֹ, וְאֵלּוּ הֵן:

פֶּסַח, מַצָּה וּמָרוֹר:

(Lift the Zeroa for all to see, and say)

Leader : פֶּסַח שֶׁהָיוּ אֲבוֹתֵינוּ אוֹכְלִים, בִּזְמַן שֶׁבֵּית הַמִּקְדָּשׁ הָיָה קַיָּם, עַל שׁוּם מָה?

All : עַל שׁוּם שֶׁפָּסַח הַקָּדוֹשׁ בָּרוּךְ הוּא, עַל בָּתֵּי אֲבוֹתֵינוּ בְּמִצְרַיִם, שֶׁנֶּאֱמַר: וַאֲמַרְתֶּם זֶבַח פֶּסַח הוּא לַיְיָ, אֲשֶׁר פָּסַח עַל בָּתֵּי בְנֵי יִשְׂרָאֵל בְּמִצְרַיִם, בְּנָגְפּוֹ אֶת־מִצְרַיִם וְאֶת־בָּתֵּינוּ הִצִּיל. וַיִּקֹּד הָעָם וַיִּשְׁתַּחֲווּ.

(Lift the Matsah for all to see, and say)

Leader : מַצָּה שֶׁאָנוּ אוֹכְלִים, עַל שׁוּם מָה?

All : עַל שׁוּם שֶׁלֹּא הִסְפִּיק בְּצֵקָם שֶׁל אֲבוֹתֵינוּ לְהַחֲמִיץ, עַד שֶׁנִּגְלָה עֲלֵיהֶם מֶלֶךְ מַלְכֵי הַמְּלָכִים, הַקָּדוֹשׁ בָּרוּךְ הוּא, וּגְאָלָם, שֶׁנֶּאֱמַר: וַיֹּאפוּ אֶת־הַבָּצֵק, אֲשֶׁר הוֹצִיאוּ מִמִּצְרַיִם, עֻגֹת מַצּוֹת, כִּי לֹא חָמֵץ; כִּי גֹרְשׁוּ מִמִּצְרַיִם, וְלֹא יָכְלוּ לְהִתְמַהְמֵהַּ, וְגַם צֵדָה לֹא עָשׂוּ לָהֶם.

(Lift the Maror for all to see, and say)

Leader : מָרוֹר זֶה שֶׁאָנוּ אוֹכְלִים, עַל שׁוּם מָה?

All : עַל שׁוּם שֶׁמֵּרְרוּ הַמִּצְרִים אֶת־חַיֵּי אֲבוֹתֵינוּ בְּמִצְרַיִם, שֶׁנֶּאֱמַר: וַיְמָרְרוּ אֶת־חַיֵּיהֶם בַּעֲבֹדָה קָשָׁה, בְּחֹמֶר וּבִלְבֵנִים, וּבְכָל־עֲבֹדָה בַּשָּׂדֶה; אֵת כָּל־עֲבֹדָתָם, אֲשֶׁר עָבְדוּ בָהֶם בְּפָרֶךְ.

Leader : בְּכָל־דּוֹר וָדוֹר חַיָּב אָדָם לִרְאוֹת אֶת־עַצְמוֹ, כְּאִלּוּ הוּא יָצָא מִמִּצְרַיִם, שֶׁנֶּאֱמַר: וְהִגַּדְתָּ לְבִנְךָ בַּיּוֹם הַהוּא לֵאמֹר: בַּעֲבוּר זֶה עָשָׂה יְיָ לִי, בְּצֵאתִי מִמִּצְרָיִם. לֹא אֶת־אֲבוֹתֵינוּ בִּלְבָד, גָּאַל הַקָּדוֹשׁ בָּרוּךְ הוּא, אֶלָּא אַף אוֹתָנוּ. גָּאַל עִמָּהֶם, שֶׁנֶּאֱמַר: וְאוֹתָנוּ הוֹצִיא מִשָּׁם, לְמַעַן הָבִיא אֹתָנוּ, לָתֶת לָנוּ אֶת־הָאָרֶץ אֲשֶׁר נִשְׁבַּע לַאֲבֹתֵינוּ.

Rabbi Gamaliel used to say that anyone who has not spoken about these three things, has not fulfilled his responsibility on Passover:

The Passover Lamb, Matsah and Maror.

(Lift the Zeroa for all to see, and say)

Leader: Why is it that our fathers ate the Passover sacrifice in the days when the Temple still stood?

All: It was because the Holy One, Blessed is He, passed over the houses of our fathers in Egypt, as it is written: "It is the Passover of the Lord, who passed over the houses of the children of Israel, when they were in Egypt; when He struck the Egyptians and spared our houses. And, the people bowed themselves and worshiped."

(Lift the Matsah for all to see, and say)

Leader: What is the reason we eat this matsah?

All: It is because the King of Kings, the Holy One, revealed Himself to our fathers and redeemed them before their dough could rise, as it is written: "They baked the dough they brought out of Egypt into cakes of unleavened bread. They were driven out of Egypt, and were not permitted to delay, even for the preparation of provisions for their journey."

(Lift the Maror for all to see, and say)

Leader: Why is it that we eat these bitter herbs?

All: It is because the Egyptians made the lives of our fathers bitter when we were in Egypt, as it is written: "They made their lives bitter with hard labor, with the making of mortar and bricks, and with every kind of labor in the field; it was all done with great rigor."

Leader: Therefore, from generation to generation it is necessary for a person to see himself as if he had personally come out of Egypt, as it is written: "You shall tell your son on that day: 'This is done because of what the Lord did for me when I came out of the land of Egypt.'" It was not only our fathers whom the Holy One redeemed from slavery. We were redeemed with them, as it is written: "He took us out from there so that He might give to us the land He had promised to our forefathers."

(Lift your cup and say)

לְפִיכָךְ אֲנַחְנוּ חַיָּבִים לְהוֹדוֹת, לְהַלֵּל, לְשַׁבֵּחַ, לְפָאֵר, לְרוֹמֵם, לְהַדֵּר, לְבָרֵךְ, לְעַלֵּה וּלְקַלֵּס, לְמִי שֶׁעָשָׂה לַאֲבוֹתֵינוּ וְלָנוּ אֶת־כָּל־הַנִּסִּים הָאֵלּוּ. הוֹצִיאָנוּ מֵעַבְדוּת לְחֵרוּת, מִיָּגוֹן לְשִׂמְחָה, וּמֵאֵבֶל לְיוֹם טוֹב, וּמֵאֲפֵלָה לְאוֹר גָּדוֹל, וּמִשִּׁעְבּוּד לִגְאֻלָּה. וְנֹאמַר לְפָנָיו שִׁירָה חֲדָשָׁה! הַלְלוּיָהּ!

(Put your cup back on the table without drinking and continue)

Psalm 113

הַלְלוּיָהּ, הַלְלוּ עַבְדֵי יְיָ, הַלְלוּ אֶת שֵׁם יְיָ. יְהִי שֵׁם יְיָ מְבֹרָךְ, מֵעַתָּה וְעַד עוֹלָם. מִמִּזְרַח שֶׁמֶשׁ עַד מְבוֹאוֹ, מְהֻלָּל שֵׁם יְיָ. רָם עַל כָּל גּוֹיִם יְיָ, עַל הַשָּׁמַיִם כְּבוֹדוֹ. מִי כַּייָ אֱלֹהֵינוּ, הַמַּגְבִּיהִי לָשָׁבֶת. הַמַּשְׁפִּילִי לִרְאוֹת, בַּשָּׁמַיִם וּבָאָרֶץ. מְקִימִי מֵעָפָר דָּל, מֵאַשְׁפֹּת יָרִים אֶבְיוֹן. לְהוֹשִׁיבִי עִם נְדִיבִים, עִם נְדִיבֵי עַמּוֹ. מוֹשִׁיבִי עֲקֶרֶת הַבַּיִת, אֵם הַבָּנִים שְׂמֵחָה, הַלְלוּיָהּ.

Psalm 114

בְּצֵאת יִשְׂרָאֵל מִמִּצְרָיִם, בֵּית יַעֲקֹב מֵעַם לֹעֵז. הָיְתָה יְהוּדָה לְקָדְשׁוֹ, יִשְׂרָאֵל מַמְשְׁלוֹתָיו. הַיָּם רָאָה וַיָּנֹס, הַיַּרְדֵּן יִסֹּב לְאָחוֹר. הֶהָרִים רָקְדוּ כְאֵילִים, גְּבָעוֹת כִּבְנֵי צֹאן. מַה לְּךָ הַיָּם כִּי תָנוּס, הַיַּרְדֵּן תִּסֹּב לְאָחוֹר. הֶהָרִים תִּרְקְדוּ כְאֵילִים, גְּבָעוֹת כִּבְנֵי צֹאן. מִלִּפְנֵי אָדוֹן חוּלִי אָרֶץ, מִלִּפְנֵי אֱלוֹהַּ יַעֲקֹב. הַהֹפְכִי הַצּוּר אֲגַם מָיִם, חַלָּמִישׁ לְמַעְיְנוֹ מָיִם.

(Lift the Second Cup, and say)

בָּרוּךְ אַתָּה יְיָ, אֱלֹהֵינוּ מֶלֶךְ הָעוֹלָם, אֲשֶׁר גְּאָלָנוּ וְגָאַל אֶת־אֲבוֹתֵינוּ מִמִּצְרַיִם, וְהִגִּיעָנוּ לַלַּיְלָה הַזֶּה, לֶאֱכָל־בּוֹ מַצָּה וּמָרוֹר. כֵּן, יְיָ אֱלֹהֵינוּ וֵאלֹהֵי אֲבוֹתֵינוּ, יַגִּיעֵנוּ לְמוֹעֲדִים וְלִרְגָלִים אֲחֵרִים, הַבָּאִים לִקְרָאתֵנוּ לְשָׁלוֹם. שְׂמֵחִים בְּבִנְיַן עִירֶךָ, וְשָׂשִׂים בַּעֲבוֹדָתֶךָ, וְנֹאכַל שָׁם מִן הַזְּבָחִים וּמִן הַפְּסָחִים, אֲשֶׁר יַגִּיעַ דָּמָם, עַל קִיר מִזְבַּחֲךָ לְרָצוֹן, וְנוֹדֶה לְּךָ שִׁיר חָדָשׁ עַל גְּאֻלָּתֵנוּ, וְעַל פְּדוּת נַפְשֵׁנוּ. בָּרוּךְ אַתָּה יְיָ, גָּאַל יִשְׂרָאֵל.

בָּרוּךְ אַתָּה יְיָ אֱלֹהֵינוּ מֶלֶךְ הָעוֹלָם, בּוֹרֵא פְּרִי הַגָּפֶן.

Barukh atah Adonai Eloheinu Melekh Ha'Olam, borei p'ri ha'gafen.

(Drink the Second Cup leaning to the left)

(Lift your cup and say)

Therefore, it is our responsibility to thank, praise, laud, glorify, extol, honor, bless, exalt, and proclaim Him who performed these wonders for our fathers, and for us. He brought us from slavery to freedom; from anguish to joy; from mourning to festivity; from darkness to great light. Therefore, we will recite a new song to Him who brought our redemption! Halleluyah!

(Put your cup back on the table without drinking and continue)

Psalm 113

Praise the Lord. Praise Him, you the servants of the Lord. Praise the name of the Lord. Blessed be the name of the Lord, from this time forth and forever more. From the rising of the sun unto the going down of the same, the Lord's name is to be praised. The Lord is high above all nations and His glory is above the heavens. Who is like the Lord our God, whose seat is lifted up, yet humbles Himself to behold the things that are in heaven and in the earth? He raises up the poor out of the dust, and lifts up the needy from the dirt, that He may set him with princes, even with the princes of His people. He makes the barren woman to keep house, and to be a joyful mother of children. Praise the Lord.

Psalm 114

When Israel went out from Egypt, the house of Jacob from a people of strange language, Judah became His sanctuary, Israel His dominion. The sea saw it, and fled; the Jordan was driven back. The mountains skipped like rams and the little hills like lambs. What ails you, oh sea, that you flee? You Jordan, that you turn back? You mountains, that you skip like rams, you little hills like lambs? Tremble, all the earth, at the presence of the Lord, at the presence of the God of Jacob, who turned the rock into a pool of water, the flint into a fountain of waters.

(Lift the Second Cup, and say)

Blessed are you, Lord our God, King of the Universe, who has redeemed us and our fathers from Egypt. You have enabled us to reach this night that we might eat matsah and bitter herbs. Therefore, Lord our God, and God of our fathers, enable us to reach the other holy days and festivals in peace. We rejoice in the building of Your City; we are joyful to serve You. In that place we shall partake in the offerings and sacrifices which will be rightly placed upon Your altar. We shall sing a new song of praise to You for our redemption and for the deliverance of our soul. Blessed are You, Lord, who has redeemed Israel.

Blessed are You, Lord our God, King of the Universe, who creates the fuit of the vine.

(Drink the Second Cup leaning to the left)

Just as the first cup of wine is called the Cup of Sanctification, this second cup is called the Cup of Judgment. It must be acknowledged that while God did indeed take us out of Egyptian bondage, the thinking, lifestyle and attitude of 400 years of slavery left their mark on us. God in His mercy promised that He would judge and remove slavery's influence from us. Even today, God is the same. If we come to Him, He will make us free from the bondage of sin and death which have held us all, and He will slowly but surely remove those habits and sins that so easily beset us. As with everything else, even in God's judgment He is merciful to those who love and humbly seek Him.

רחצה

(Wash the hands, and say)

בָּרוּךְ אַתָּה יְיָ אֱלֹהֵינוּ מֶלֶךְ הָעוֹלָם, אֲשֶׁר קִדְּשָׁנוּ בְּמִצְוֹתָיו, וְצִוָּנוּ עַל נְטִילַת יָדָיִם.

Barukh atah Adonai, Eloheinu Melekh Ha'Olam, asher kid'shanu b'mitsvotav, v'tsivanu al netilat yadayim.

מוציא מצה

(While the Leader of the Seder holds the remaining matsot together from the Matsah Tosh, the two blessings below are recited. After this everyone at the table takes at least an olive-sized piece of this matsah from the Matsah Tosh)

בָּרוּךְ אַתָּה יְיָ אֱלֹהֵינוּ מֶלֶךְ הָעוֹלָם, הַמּוֹצִיא לֶחֶם מִן הָאָרֶץ.

Barukh atah Adonai Eloheinu Melekh Ha'Olam, hamotsi leḥem min ha'arets.

בָּרוּךְ אַתָּה יְיָ, אֱלֹהֵינוּ מֶלֶךְ הָעוֹלָם, אֲשֶׁר קִדְּשָׁנוּ בְּמִצְוֹתָיו, וְצִוָּנוּ עַל אֲכִילַת מַצָּה.

Barukh atah Adonai Eloheinu Melekh Ha'Olam, asher kid'shanu b'mitsvotav, v'tsivanu al akhilat matsah.

(Eat the matsah while reclining to the left)

מרור-חזרת

(Eat a small amount of maror or ḥazeret dipped into the ḥaroset or on a piece of matsah, and recite the following blessing before eating without reclining)

בָּרוּךְ אַתָּה יְיָ אֱלֹהֵינוּ מֶלֶךְ הָעוֹלָם, אֲשֶׁר קִדְּשָׁנוּ בְּמִצְוֹתָיו, וְצִוָּנוּ עַל אֲכִילַת מָרוֹר.

Barukh atah Adonai Eloheinu Melekh Ha'Olam, asher kid'shanu b'mitsvotav, v'tsivanu al akhilat maror.

כרך

(Make an open sandwich of either ḥazeret or maror with ḥaroset on matsah and eat it without a blessing while reclining to the left after reciting the following statement)

זֵכֶר לְמִקְדָּשׁ כְּהִלֵּל. כֵּן עָשָׂה הִלֵּל בִּזְמַן שֶׁבֵּית הַמִּקְדָּשׁ הָיָה קַיָּם.

ביצה (חגיגה)

(Dip a piece of hardboiled egg into salt water and eat it without a blessing in remembrance of the additional festival sacrifice)

שלחן עורך

Raḥtsah

(Wash the hands, and say)

Blessed are You, Lord our God, King of the Universe, who has sanctified us with His commandments and has commanded us regarding washing our hands.

Motsi Matsah

(While the Leader of the Seder holds the remaining matsot together from the Matsah Tosh, the two blessings below are recited. After this everyone at the table takes at least an olive-sized piece of this matsah from the Matsah Tosh)

Blessed are You Lord our God, King of the Universe, who brings forth bread from the earth.

Blessed are You, Lord our God, King of the Universe, who has set us apart through His commandments, and who has commanded us concerning eating matsah.

(Eat the matsah while reclining to the left)

Maror – Ḥazeret

(Eat a small amount of maror or ḥazeret dipped into the ḥaroset or on a piece of matsah, and recite the following blessing before eating without reclining)

Blessed are You, Lord our God, King of the Universe, who has set us apart through His commandments, and who has commanded us concerning eating bitter herbs.

Korekh

(Make an open sandwich of either ḥazeret or maror with ḥaroset on matsah and eat it without a blessing while reclining to the left after reciting the following statement)

In memory of the Temple according to Hillel. This is what Hillel would do when the Temple existed.

Beitsah (Ḥagigah)

(Dip a piece of hardboiled egg into salt water and eat it without a blessing in remembrance of the additional festival sacrifice)

The Festival Meal

צפון

(After everyone is completely satisfied from the meal, the Afikoman is searched for and must be found. The Afikoman is then broken into pieces at least the size of an olive and distributed to all at the table)

Leader : זֵכֶר לְקָרְבַּן פֶּסַח הַנֶּאֱכַל עַל הַשּׂוֹבַע.

Leader : לָקַח אֶת הַלֶּחֶם, בֵּרֵךְ וּבָצַע וְנָתַן לָהֶם בְּאָמְרוֹ: "זֶה גּוּפִי הַנִּתָּן בַּעַדְכֶם, זֹאת עֲשׂוּ לְזִכְרִי."

(Recite the following blessing remembering Messiah Yeshua's sacrifice as our ultimate Passover Lamb)

בָּרוּךְ אַתָּה יְיָ אֱלֹהֵינוּ מֶלֶךְ הָעוֹלָם, אֲשֶׁר קִדְּשָׁנוּ בְּמִצְוֹתָיו, וְצִוָּנוּ לִזְכּוֹר הַלֶּחֶם הַחַי, מְשִׁיחֵנוּ יֵשׁוּעַ.

Barukh atah Adonai, Eloheinu Melekh Ha'Olam, asher kid'shanu b'mitsvotav, v'tsivanu liz'kor HaLeḥem HaḤai, Meshiḥeinu Yeishua.

(Eat the Afikoman reclining to the left, soberly reflecting on Messiah Yeshua's death)

(No other food is to be eaten after this point of the Seder)

Tsaphoon

(After everyone is completely satisfied from the meal, the Afikoman is searched for and must be found. The Afikoman is then broken into pieces at least the size of an olive and distributed to all at the table)

Leader: In memory of the Passover sacrifice that was eaten only after one was no longer hungry.

Leader: And taking the matsah, he gave the blessing, broke it, and said, "This is my body which is being broken for you. As often as you do this, do this in remembrance of me."

(Recite the following blessing remembering Messiah Yeshua's sacrifice as our ultimate Passover Lamb)

All: Blessed are You, Lord our God, King of the Universe, who sanctifies us by His commandments and has commanded us to remember the Bread of Life, our Messiah Yeshua.

(Eat the Afikoman reclining to the left, soberly reflecting on Messiah Yeshua's death)

(No other food is to be eaten after this point of the Seder)

There are many traditions that surround the three matsot of the Matsah Tosh, the breaking of the middle matsah and the Afikoman. Our current Seder tradition seems to have developed long after the destruction of the Temple and for reasons that are not clearly known.

The Passover Meal before the Temple's destruction in 70 CE, as we wrote in the introduction, does not seem to have had the clear order that we read about in the Mishnah and Tosefta of the late second century. Even then, there is little information provided about the elements and whether some of today's Seder elements were even used during the first century meal. The very meaning of the word, ***Afikoman***, is a mystery itself, some understanding it as "Dessert", and others as "The Coming One". Some speculate that the Jewish community of Yeshua followers added some elements, such as the breaking of the middle matsah and the Afikoman. These customs do seem to relate to the person of the Messiah who was sent forth from God to be broken by and for us, as well as the eating of a small piece of matsah in remembrance of the lamb after the meal. Yes, the body of the Messiah was wrapped in a burial cloth and hidden away. Yes, Yeshua's followers went to anoint His body and found it missing. And yes, Messiah Yeshua rose from the dead on the third day after his burial and appeared to his talmidim. But there is no evidence that Messiah Yeshua's Seder included three matsot, with the middle matsah removed, broken and wrapped in a cloth. According to Mishnah Pesachim, chapter 10, there was no Afikoman; it was prohibited in the days of the Temple. Instead a small piece of the Passover lamb was eaten ritually after the meal in rememberance of the first Passover lamb from Egypt, after which no other solid food was to be eaten. It is quite possible that after the eating of this small piece of lamb, assuming this was indeed a common Passover ritual in the first century, Messiah Yeshua might then have used broken matsah as a way to ritualize remembrance of his death providing freedom from slavery to sin.We just don't know for sure because there is not enough clear textual evidence.

At Passover, all of us as Jews will take a final piece of matsah after the meal in remembrance of a lamb. As Jewish followers of Messiah Yeshua, let us take this piece of matsah in remembrance not just of the Passover Lamb from Egypt, but more importantly in remembrance of our ultimate Passover Lamb, Messiah Yeshua, who died as our sacrifice so that we could have forgiveness for our sins and a relationship with God.

ברך

(Fill the Third Cup)

שִׁיר הַמַּעֲלוֹת. בְּשׁוּב יְיָ אֶת שִׁיבַת צִיּוֹן הָיִינוּ כְּחֹלְמִים. אָז יִמָּלֵא שְׂחוֹק פִּינוּ, וּלְשׁוֹנֵנוּ רִנָּה; אָז יֹאמְרוּ בַגּוֹיִם, הִגְדִּיל יְיָ לַעֲשׂוֹת עִם אֵלֶּה. הִגְדִּיל יְיָ לַעֲשׂוֹת עִמָּנוּ, הָיִינוּ שְׂמֵחִים. שׁוּבָה יְיָ אֶת שְׁבִיתֵנוּ, כַּאֲפִיקִים בַּנֶּגֶב. הַזֹּרְעִים בְּדִמְעָה, בְּרִנָּה יִקְצֹרוּ. הָלוֹךְ יֵלֵךְ וּבָכֹה נֹשֵׂא מֶשֶׁךְ הַזָּרַע; בֹּא יָבוֹא בְרִנָּה נֹשֵׂא אֲלֻמֹּתָיו.

Shir Hama'alot, b'shuv Adonai et shivat Tsiyon hayinu k'ḥol'mim. Az yimalei s'ḥok pinu ul'shoneinu rinah. Az yom'ru vagoyim higdil Adonai la'asot im eileh. Higdil Adonai la'asot imanu hayinu s'meiḥim. Shuvah Adonai et sheviteinu, ka'afikim banegev. Hazor'im b'dimah, b'rinah yik'tsoru. Halokh Yeileikh uvakhoh noseih meshekh haza'ra, bo yavo v'rinah nosei alumotayv.

(Recite the zimmun if three or more have eaten together. Text in parentheses are recited with a minyan. The Leader selected by the group begins the zimmun)

חֲבֵרַי נְבָרֵךְ.

Ḥaveiray n'vareikh!

(Those around the table respond)

יְהִי שֵׁם יְיָ מְבֹרָךְ מֵעַתָּה וְעַד עוֹלָם.

Y'hi sheim Adonai m'vorakh mei-atah v'ad olam.

(The Leader says)

יְהִי שֵׁם יְיָ מְבֹרָךְ מֵעַתָּה וְעַד עוֹלָם. בִּרְשׁוּת חֲבֵרַי, נְבָרֵךְ (אֱלֹהֵינוּ) שֶׁאָכַלְנוּ מִשֶּׁלּוֹ.

Y'hi sheim Adonai m'vorakh mei-atah v'ad olam.
Birshut ḥaveiray, n'vareikh (Eloheinu) she-akha-lenu mishelo.

(Those around the table respond and then the Leader repeats)

בָּרוּךְ (אֱלֹהֵינוּ) שֶׁאָכַלְנוּ מִשֶּׁלּוֹ וּבְטוּבוֹ חָיִינוּ.

Barukh (Eloheinu) she-akha-lenu mishelo uv'tuvo ḥayinu.

(Together)

בָּרוּךְ הוּא וּבָרוּךְ שְׁמוֹ.

Barukh hu uvarukh sh'mo

Barekh

(Fill the Third Cup)

A Song of Ascents. When the Lord restored the fortunes of Tsiyon, we were like those who dream. Then our mouth was filled with laughter, and our tongue with shouts of joy; then they said among the nations, "The Lord has done great things for them." The Lord has done great things for us; we are glad. Restore our fortunes, O Lord, like the streams in the Negeb! May those who sow in tears reap with shouts of joy! He that goes forth weeping, bearing the seed for sowing, shall come home with shouts of joy, bringing his sheaves with him.

(Recite the zimmun if three or more have eaten together. Text in parentheses are recited with a minyan. The Leader selected by the group begins the zimmun)

Friends, let us give blessing!

(Those around the table respond)

May the Name of the Lord be blessed both now and forever!

(The Leader says)

May the Name of the Lord be blessed both now and forever! With your permission Friends, let us shout with joy, (blessing God) for the bounty we have shared.

(Those around the table respond and then the Leader repeats)

Blessed (is our God), for the bounty we have shared, and whose goodness is upon our life.

(Together)

Blessed is He and blessed is His Name!

בָּרוּךְ אַתָּה יְיָ, אֱלֹהֵינוּ מֶלֶךְ הָעוֹלָם, הַזָּן אֶת הָעוֹלָם כֻּלּוֹ בְּטוּבוֹ בְּחֵן בְּחֶסֶד וּבְרַחֲמִים. הוּא נוֹתֵן לֶחֶם לְכָל בָּשָׂר כִּי לְעוֹלָם חַסְדּוֹ. וּבְטוּבוֹ הַגָּדוֹל תָּמִיד לֹא חָסַר לָנוּ, וְאַל יֶחְסַר לָנוּ מָזוֹן לְעוֹלָם וָעֶד, בַּעֲבוּר שְׁמוֹ הַגָּדוֹל. כִּי הוּא אֵל זָן וּמְפַרְנֵס לַכֹּל וּמֵטִיב לַכֹּל. וּמֵכִין מָזוֹן לְכֹל בְּרִיּוֹתָיו אֲשֶׁר בָּרָא. בָּרוּךְ אַתָּה יְיָ, הַזָּן אֶת הַכֹּל.

Barukh atah Adonai, Eloheinu Melekh haolam, hazan et ha-olam kulo b'tuvo, b'ḥein b'ḥesed uv'raḥamim. Hu notein leḥem l'khol basar ki l'olam ḥasdo. Uv'tuvo hagadol tamid lo ḥasar lanu, v'al yeḥsar lanu, mazon l'olam va-ed, baavur sh'mo hagadol. Ki hu Eil zan um'farneis lakol umeitiv lakol, umeikhin mazon l'khol b'riyotav asher bara. Barukh atah Adonai, hazan et hakol.

נוֹדֶה לְּךָ יְיָ אֱלֹהֵינוּ עַל שֶׁהִנְחַלְתָּ לַאֲבוֹתֵינוּ, אֶרֶץ חֶמְדָּה טוֹבָה וּרְחָבָה. בְּרִית וְתוֹרָה, חַיִּים וּמָזוֹן. יִתְבָּרַךְ שִׁמְךָ בְּפִי כָּל חַי תָּמִיד לְעוֹלָם וָעֶד. כַּכָּתוּב, וְאָכַלְתָּ וְשָׂבָעְתָּ, וּבֵרַכְתָּ אֶת יְיָ אֱלֹהֶיךָ עַל הָאָרֶץ הַטֹּבָה אֲשֶׁר נָתַן לָךְ. בָּרוּךְ אַתָּה יְיָ, עַל הָאָרֶץ וְעַל הַמָּזוֹן.

Nodeh l'ka, Adonai Eloheinu, al shehin'ḥa'leta laavoteinu,
erets ḥemdah tovah ur'ḥavah; b'rit v'Torah, ḥayim u'mazon.
Yit'barakh shim'ka b'fi kol ḥai tamid l'olam va-ed.
Kakatuv, v'akhal'ta v'sava'ta, uveirakhta et Adonai Eloheka al haarets hatovah asher natan lakh. Barukh atah Adonai, al haarets v'al hamazon.

(On Shabbat add)

רְצֵה וְהַחֲלִיצֵנוּ יְיָ אֱלֹהֵינוּ בְּמִצְוֹתֶיךָ וּבְמִצְוַת יוֹם הַשְּׁבִיעִי הַשַּׁבָּת הַגָּדוֹל וְהַקָּדוֹשׁ הַזֶּה. כִּי יוֹם זֶה גָּדוֹל וְקָדוֹשׁ הוּא לְפָנֶיךָ. לִשְׁבָּת בּוֹ וְלָנוּחַ בּוֹ בְּאַהֲבָה כְּמִצְוַת רְצוֹנֶךָ וּבִרְצוֹנְךָ הָנִיחַ לָנוּ יְיָ אֱלֹהֵינוּ, שֶׁלֹּא תְהֵא צָרָה וְיָגוֹן וַאֲנָחָה בְּיוֹם מְנוּחָתֵנוּ. וְהַרְאֵנוּ יְיָ אֱלֹהֵינוּ בְּנֶחָמַת צִיּוֹן עִירֶךָ, וּבְבִנְיַן יְרוּשָׁלַיִם עִיר קָדְשֶׁךָ, כִּי אַתָּה הוּא בַּעַל הַיְשׁוּעוֹת וּבַעַל הַנֶּחָמוֹת.

R'tsei v'haḥalitsei'nu Adonai Eloheinu b'mitsvotekha uv'mitsvat yom hash'vi'i haShabbat hagadol v'hakadosh hazeh. Ki yom zeh gadol v'kadosh hu l'fane-kha. Lish'bat bo v'lanuaḥ bo b'ahavah k'mitsvat r'tsonekha uvir'tson'kha hani'aḥ lanu Adonai Eloheinu, shelo t'hei tsarah v'yagon va'anaḥeh b'yom m'nuḥateinu. V'har'ei'nu Adonai Eloheinu b'neḥamat Tsiyon irekha, uv'vinyan Y'rushalayim ir kad'shekha, ki atah hu ba'al hay'shuot uva'al haneḥamot.

Blessed are You, Lord our God, King of the Universe, who, through His goodness, nourishes the whole world with grace, loving kindness and compassion. Indeed, "He gives bread to all flesh because His loving kindness endures forever." His great goodness, with which we are sustained, has never diminished toward us; nor will it ever, for the sake of His great Name. He is God who provides nourishment for all, and who does good to all. He provides food for all His creation. Blessed are You, Lord, who provides food for all.

And besides all these things, Lord our God, we give You thanks and bless You for Your miracles. Your Name will be magnified by the mouth of all who live, forever and to all eternity. As it is written, "You shall eat and be satisfied, and give blessing to the Lord your God for the good land He has given to you." Blessed are You, Lord, for the land and for its produce.

(On Shabbat add)
Lord our God, may You take pleasure in strengthening us through all Your commandments and in the command concerning the seventh day, this great and holy Shabbat. For before Your countenance, this day is great and holy; that we might dwell in Your rest and in Your love, in keeping with the desire of Your command. And may it be Your will, Lord our God, to grant us such rest; that there be no misfortune, or grief, or sighing on the day of our rest. Lord our God, may we behold Tsiyon Your city being comforted, and our descendents in Jerusalem Your holy city, for You are the Master of all salvation, and the Master of all consolation.

אֱלֹהֵינוּ וֵאלֹהֵי אֲבוֹתֵינוּ, יַעֲלֶה וְיָבֹא וְיַגִּיעַ, וְיֵרָאֶה, וְיֵרָצֶה, וְיִשָּׁמַע,
וְיִפָּקֵד, וְיִזָּכֵר זִכְרוֹנֵנוּ וּפִקְדוֹנֵנוּ, וְזִכְרוֹן אֲבוֹתֵינוּ, וְזִכְרוֹן מָשִׁיחַ
יֵשׁוּעַ בֶּן דָּוִד עַבְדֶּךָ, וְזִכְרוֹן יְרוּשָׁלַיִם עִיר קָדְשֶׁךָ, וְזִכְרוֹן כָּל עַמְּךָ
בֵּית יִשְׂרָאֵל לְפָנֶיךָ, לִפְלֵיטָה לְטוֹבָה לְחֵן וּלְחֶסֶד וּלְרַחֲמִים, לְחַיִּים
וּלְשָׁלוֹם בְּיוֹם חַג הַמַּצּוֹת הַזֶּה. זָכְרֵנוּ יְיָ אֱלֹהֵינוּ בּוֹ לְטוֹבָה.
וּפָקְדֵנוּ בוֹ לִבְרָכָה, וְהוֹשִׁיעֵנוּ בוֹ לְחַיִּים. וּבִדְבַר יְשׁוּעָה וְרַחֲמִים,
חוּס וְחָנֵּנוּ, וְרַחֵם עָלֵינוּ וְהוֹשִׁיעֵנוּ. כִּי אֵלֶיךָ עֵינֵינוּ, כִּי אֵל מֶלֶךְ
חַנּוּן וְרַחוּם אָתָּה.

Eloheinu ve-Elohei Avoteinu, ya'aleh ve-yavo ve-yagi'a, ve-yeira'eh, ve-yeiratseh, ve-yishama, ve-yipakeid, ve-yizakheir zikh'roneinu u-fik'doneinu, ve-zikh'ron avoteinu, ve-zikh'ron Mashi'aḥ Yeishua ben David av'dekha, ve-zikh'ron Yerushalayim ir kod'shekha, ve-zikh'ron kol am'kha beit Yisra'el lefanekha, li-f'leitah le-tovah, le- ḥein u-le-ḥesed u-le-raḥamim, le-ḥayim u-le-shalom, be-yom Hag ha-Matsot ha-zeh. Zokh'reinu, Adonai Eloheinu, boh le-tovah. U-fokdeinu voh li-v'rakhah, ve-hoshi'einu voh le-ḥayim. U-vid'var yeishuah ve-raḥamim, ḥus ve-ḥaneinu, ve-raḥeim aleinu ve-hoshi'einu. Ki eilekha eineinu, ki El Melekh ḥanun ve-raḥum atah.

וּבְנֵה יְרוּשָׁלַיִם עִיר הַקֹּדֶשׁ בִּמְהֵרָה בְיָמֵינוּ. בָּרוּךְ אַתָּה יְיָ, בּוֹנֵה
בְרַחֲמָיו יְרוּשָׁלָיִם. אָמֵן.

*Uv'neih Y'rushalayim ir hakodesh bimheirah v'yameinu.
Barukh atah Adonai, boneih v'raḥamav Y'rushalayim. Amein.*

בָּרוּךְ אַתָּה יְיָ אֱלֹהֵינוּ מֶלֶךְ הָעוֹלָם, הַמֶּלֶךְ הַטּוֹב, וְהַמֵּטִיב לַכֹּל,
הוּא הֵטִיב, הוּא מֵטִיב, הוּא יֵיטִיב לָנוּ. הוּא גְמָלָנוּ, הוּא גוֹמְלֵנוּ,
הוּא יִגְמְלֵנוּ לָעַד לְחֵן וּלְחֶסֶד וּלְרַחֲמִים. וּמִכָּל טוּב לְעוֹלָם אַל
יְחַסְּרֵנוּ.

Barukh atah Adonai Eloheinu Melekh Ha'Olam, HaMelekh hatov v'hameitiv lakol, hu heitiv, hu meitiv, hu yeitiv lanu. Hu g'malanu, hu gom'leinu, hu yigm'leinu la'ad l'ḥein ul'ḥesed ul'raḥamim, umikal tuv l'olam al y'ḥas'reinu.

Our God, and God of our fathers, may the remembrance and the consideration of us, and the remembrance of our fathers, and the remembrance of Messiah Yeshua, the son of David Your servant, and the remembrance of Jerusalem Your holy city, and the remembrance of all Your people, the House of Israel, arise and come, and reach, and be seen, and be accepted, and be heard, and be numbered, and be remembered before Your face; for deliverance, for favor, for grace and for loving kindness, and for compassion, and for peace on this day of the Festival of Unleavened Bread. Lord our God, remember us for goodness. Command blessing for us, and save us that we might live. Concerning salvation and compassion, take pity and pardon us, and have compassion on us, for You are our salvation. Our eyes are lifted to You, for You, God, are a gracious and compassionate King.

Rebuild Jerusalem as a holy city very soon, even in our day. Blessed are You, Lord, who, in compassion, builds Jerusalem. Amen.

Blessed are You, Lord our God, King of the Universe, the Good King who is good to all. He has done good, and He continually does good for us. He has dealt bountifully with us, He deals bountifully with us, and He will always deal bountifully with us; for grace, and for loving kindness, and for compassion. May God, who knows our need, always provide us with good.

(On Shabbat say)

הָרַחֲמָן, הוּא יַנְחִילֵנוּ יוֹם שֶׁכֻּלּוֹ שַׁבָּת וּמְנוּחָה לְחַיֵּי הָעוֹלָמִים.

Harahaman, hu yan'ḥileinu yom she-kulo Shabbat um'nuḥah l'ḥayeiy ha-olamim.

(On other days continue here)

הָרַחֲמָן, הוּא יְבָרֵךְ אֶת־מְדִינַת יִשְׂרָאֵל, רֵאשִׁית צְמִיחַת גְּאֻלָּתֵנוּ.

Harahaman, hu y'vareikh et M'dinat Yisraeil, reishit ts'miḥat g'u-lateinu.

הָרַחֲמָן, הוּא יְבָרֵךְ אֶת־אַחֵינוּ בְּנֵי יִשְׂרָאֵל הַנְּתוּנִים בְּצָרָה,
וְיוֹצִיאֵם מֵאֲפֵלָה לְאוֹרָה.

Harahaman, hu y'vareikh et aḥeinu b'nei Yisraeil han'tunim b'tsarah, v'yotsi-eim mei-afeilah l'orah.

הָרַחֲמָן, הוּא יְזַכֵּנוּ לִימוֹת הַמָּשִׁיחַ יֵשׁוּעַ וּלְחַיֵּי הָעוֹלָם הַבָּא.

Harahaman, hu y'zakeinu limot haMashiaḥ Yeishua ul'ḥayeiy ha-olam haba.

מִגְדּוֹל יְשׁוּעוֹת מַלְכּוֹ, וְעֹשֶׂה חֶסֶד לִמְשִׁיחוֹ לְדָוִד וּלְזַרְעוֹ עַד עוֹלָם.
עֹשֶׂה שָׁלוֹם בִּמְרוֹמָיו, הוּא יַעֲשֶׂה שָׁלוֹם, עָלֵינוּ וְעַל כָּל יִשְׂרָאֵל,
וְאִמְרוּ, אָמֵן.

Migdol y'shuot malko, v'oseh ḥesed lim'shiḥo l'David ul'zaro ad olam. Oseh shalom bim'romayv, hu ya'aseh shalom, aleinu v'al kal Yisraeil, v'im-ru amein.

(On Shabbat say)
The Compassionate One, may He cause us to come to that day which shall always be Shabbat, with rest in life everlasting.

(On other days continue here)
The Compassionate One, may He bless the State of Israel, the dawn of our redemption.

The Compassionate One, may He bless all of our people Israel who suffer, and bring them out of darkness into light.

The Compassionate One, may He declare us worthy of Messiah Yeshua and life in the world to come.

He fortifies the salvation of His Kingship, and shows loving kindness to His anointed, to David and to his seed forever. May He who creates peace in the high heavens, may He create peace for us, and for all Israel, and let us say amen.

Leader: Now on the morning before the Festival of Unleavened Bread the talmidim came to Yeshua, and said to him, "Where do you want us to prepare for you to eat the Passover?" And he said, "Go into the city to a certain man, and say to him, 'The Rabbi says, "My time is at hand; I will keep the Passover at your house with my talmidim.'" So the talmidim did as Yeshua had directed them; and they prepared the Passover. When evening had come, he sat down with his twelve talmidim, and as they were eating, he said, "I tell you the truth, one of you will betray me." And they were very upset, and each of them began to say to him, "Lord, is it me?" He answered and said, "He who dipped his hand with me in the dish will betray me. The Son of Man indeed goes just as it is written of him, but woe to that person by whom the Son of Man is betrayed! It would have been better for them if they had not been born." Then Judah, who was betraying him, answered and said, "Rabbi, is it me?" He said to him, "You have said it." And as they were eating, Yeshua took bread, blessed and broke it, and gave it to the talmidim and said, "Take, eat; this is my body." Then he took the cup after they had eaten the meal, and gave thanks, and gave it to them, saying, "Drink from it, all of you. This is the blood of the New Covenant, which is shed for many for the forgiveness of sins. But I say to you, I will not drink of this fruit of the vine from now on until the day when I will drink it with you in my Father's kingdom." And when they had sung the Hallel, they went out to the Mount of Olives.

All: Then Yeshua came with them to a place called Gethsemane, and said to the talmidim, "Sit here while I go and pray over there." And he took with him Simon and the two sons of Zebedee, and he began to be filled with sorrow and he was deeply distressed. Then he said to them, "My soul is exceedingly troubled, even to death. Stay here and pray with me." He went a little farther and fell on his face, and prayed, saying, "O my Father, if it is possible, let this cup pass from me; nevertheless, not as I will, but as You will." Then he came to the talmidim and found them sleeping, and said to Simon, "What! Could you not pray with me one hour? Watch and pray, lest you enter into temptation. The spirit indeed is willing, but the flesh is weak." He went away again and prayed, saying, "My Father, if this cup cannot pass away from me unless I drink it, Your will be done." He returned to the talmidim and found them asleep again, for they were very tired. So he left them, went away again, and prayed the third time, saying the same words. Finally, he came to his talmidim and said to them, "Are you still sleeping and resting? Behold, the hour is at hand, and the Son of Man is being betrayed into the hands of sinners. Rise up, let us be going. See, my betrayer is here."

Leader: And while he was still speaking, Judah (one of his talmidim) along with a great crowd of men carrying swords and clubs, came from the chief priests and elders of the people. Now his betrayer had given them a sign, saying, "Whomever I kiss, he is the one; seize him." Immediately he went up to Yeshua and said, "Greetings, Rabbi!" and kissed him. Yeshua said to him, "Friend, why have you come?" Then they came and laid hands on Yeshua and took him.

All: Now Yeshua stood before the governor, and the governor asked him, "Are you the King of the Jews?" Yeshua said to him, "It is as you say." But, while he was being accused by the chief priests and elders, he answered nothing. So Pilate said to him, "Do you not hear how many things they testify against you?" But Yeshua did not defend himself at all, so the governor was confused.

Leader: The soldiers of the governor took Yeshua into the Praetorium and gathered the whole garrison around him. There they stripped him and put a scarlet robe on him. When they had twisted a crown of thorns, they pushed it down on his head and placed a reed in his right hand. Then, they bowed the knee before him and mocked him, saying, "Hail, King of the Jews!" Then they spat on him, and took the reed and struck him on the head. And when they had mocked him, they took the robe off him, put his own clothes back on him, and led him away to be crucified.

All: When they had come to a place called Golgotha, which means "Place of a Skull", they crucified him, and divided his garments, casting lots, that it might be fulfilled which was spoken by the prophet: "*They divided my garments among them, and for my clothing they cast lots.*" Sitting down, they kept watch over him there. And they put up over his head the accusation written against him: ***This is Yeshua, the King of the Jews.***

Leader: Now from the sixth hour until the ninth hour there was darkness over the land, and around the ninth hour Yeshua cried out with a loud voice, saying, "Eli, Eli, lama ah-sahv-tahnee?" that is, *"My God, my God, why have You forsaken me?"* Some of those who stood there, when they heard that, said, "This man is calling for Elijah!" Immediately one of them ran and took a sponge, filled it with sour wine and put it on a reed, and offered it to him to drink. The rest said, "Let him alone; let us see if Elijah will come to save him." Suddenly, Yeshua cried out with a loud voice saying, "It is finished!" and died.

All: Indeed, Messiah Yeshua, our Passover, was sacrificed for us!

1 Corinthians 11:25-26

כֵּן גַּם לָקַח יֵשׁוּעַ אֶת הַכּוֹס לְאַחַר הַסְּעוּדָה וְאָמַר: "הַכּוֹס הַזֹּאת הִיא הַבְּרִית הַחֲדָשָׁה בְּדָמִי, זֹאת עֲשׂוּ לְזִכְרִי בְּכָל עֵת שֶׁתִּשְׁתּוּ." הֵן בְּכָל עֵת שֶׁאַתֶּם אוֹכְלִים אֶת הַלֶּחֶם הַזֶּה וְשׁוֹתִים מִן הַכּוֹס הַזֹּאת, אַתֶּם מַזְכִּירִים אֶת מוֹת אֲדוֹנֵנוּ, עַד שֶׁיָּבוֹא.

(Lift the Third Cup, and say)

בָּרוּךְ אַתָּה יְיָ אֱלֹהֵינוּ מֶלֶךְ הָעוֹלָם, בּוֹרֵא פְּרִי הַגָּפֶן.

Barukh atah Adonai Eloheinu Melekh Ha'Olam, borei p'ri ha'gafen.

(Recite the following blessing remembering Messiah Yeshua's sacrifice as our ultimate Passover Lamb)

בָּרוּךְ אַתָּה יְיָ אֱלֹהֵינוּ מֶלֶךְ הָעוֹלָם, אֲשֶׁר קִדְּשָׁנוּ בְּמִצְוֹתָיו, וְצִוָּנוּ לִזְכּוֹר דַּם הַבְּרִית מְשִׁיחֵנוּ יֵשׁוּעַ.

Barukh atah Adonai, Eloheinu Melekh Ha'Olam, asher kid'shanu b'mitsvotav, v'tsivanu liz'kor Dam HaBrit Meshiḥeinu Yeishua.

(Drink the Third Cup reclining to the left, while soberly reflecting on Messiah Yeshua's death providing the atonement for your sin)

(Fill the Fourth Cup. All rise and open the door for Elijah the Prophet)

שְׁפֹךְ חֲמָתְךָ אֶל־הַגּוֹיִם, אֲשֶׁר לֹא יְדָעוּךָ וְעַל־מַמְלָכוֹת אֲשֶׁר בְּשִׁמְךָ לֹא קָרָאוּ. כִּי אָכַל אֶת־יַעֲקֹב וְאֶת־נָוֵהוּ הֵשַׁמּוּ. שְׁפָךְ־עֲלֵיהֶם זַעְמֶךָ, וַחֲרוֹן אַפְּךָ יַשִּׂיגֵם. תִּרְדֹּף בְּאַף וְתַשְׁמִידֵם, מִתַּחַת שְׁמֵי יְיָ.

(If Elijah is not there, sing Eliyahu and continue the Seder)

אֵלִיָּהוּ הַנָּבִיא, אֵלִיָּהוּ הַתִּשְׁבִּי, אֵלִיָּהוּ הַגִּלְעָדִי בִּמְהֵרָה בְיָמֵינוּ יָבֹא אֵלֵינוּ, עִם מָשִׁיחַ יֵשׁוּעַ, בֶּן דָּוִד.

Eliyahu haNavi, Eliyahu haTishbi, Eliyahu haGiladi. Bim'hera ve'yameinu yavo eileinu, im Mashiaḥ Yeishua ben David.

(Close the door and be seated)

The Prophet Elijah is understood within Jewish tradition to be the one who will announce the final judgement of the nations when Israel's Messiah comes. Messiah Yeshua alludes to this judgement of the nations in many places, but one of the most direct is in Matthew 25:31-46, where the nations that have abused his brothers, the Jewish people, will be harshly judged.

1 Corinthians 11:25-26

In the same way Yeshua took also the cup, after the meal, saying, "This cup is the New Covenant in my blood. This do, as often as you drink it, in remembrance of me." For as often as you eat this bread, and drink this cup, you proclaim our Master's death until he returns.

(Lift the Third Cup, and say)

Blessed are You, Lord our God, King of the Universe, who creates the fruit of the vine.

(Recite the following blessings remembering Messiah Yeshua's sacrifice as our ultimate Passover Lamb)

Blessed are You, Lord our God, King of the Universe, who has commanded us to remember the covenant blood of our Messiah Yeshua.

(Drink the Third Cup reclining to the left while soberly reflecting on Messiah Yeshua's death providing the atonement for your sin)

(Fill the Fourth Cup. All rise and open the door for Elijah the Prophet)

Pour out Your wrath upon the nations that do not know You and upon the kingdoms that do not call upon Your Name. They have consumed Jacob, and have laid waste his dwelling place. Bring down Your fury on them; let it overtake them. In Your anger, pursue them; destroy them from the dwelling place of the Lord.

(If Elijah is not there, sing Eliyahu and continue the Seder)

May Elijah the Prophet, Elijah of the Tishbi, Elijah of the Giladi come to us in our days proclaiming redemption, and with him Messiah Yeshua, the son of David.

(Close the door and be seated)

The Third Cup taken after the meal is traditionally taken at the conclusion of Birkat HaMazon. This is common in Jewish tradition. What is unusual is that there is evidence that in late Second Temple period tradition, additional readings related to the Passover sacrifice were added to the normal blessings, and it is possible that these additional readings more clearly related to the understanding of redemption. As we discussed earlier, a total of four specific cups are drunk, which traditionally have their meaning given from the text of Exodus 6:6-8 representing the four expressions of deliverance promised by God: "I will bring out," "I will deliver," "I will redeem," and "I will take." It is possible that it was within this context that Messiah Yeshua referred to this cup after the meal when he spoke of the sacrifice of his blood as inagurating the New Covenant promised by God in Jeremiah 31:31-34.We just don't know for sure because there is not enough remaining clear textual evidence.

At Passover, all of us as Jews will drink a third cup following the meal and after the taking of the Afikoman. As Jewish followers of Messiah Yeshua, let us drink this Third Cup in celebration of our remembrance of our ultimate Passover Lamb, Messiah Yeshua. He willingly allowed himself to be killed; he willingly allowed his blood to be shed as our atoning sacrifice. By putting our faith in his death, we receive forgiveness for our sins and as a result, peace with God.

הלל

Psalm 115:1-11

לֹא לָֽנוּ, יְיָ, לֹא לָֽנוּ, כִּי לְשִׁמְךָ תֵּן כָּבוֹד, עַל חַסְדְּךָ עַל אֲמִתֶּֽךָ. לָֽמָּה יֹאמְרוּ הַגּוֹיִם, אַיֵּה נָא אֱלֹהֵיהֶם. וֵאלֹהֵֽינוּ בַשָּׁמָֽיִם, כֹּל אֲשֶׁר חָפֵץ עָשָֽׂה. עֲצַבֵּיהֶם כֶּֽסֶף וְזָהָב, מַעֲשֵׂה יְדֵי אָדָם. פֶּה לָהֶם וְלֹא יְדַבֵּֽרוּ, עֵינַֽיִם לָהֶם וְלֹא יִרְאוּ. אָזְנַֽיִם לָהֶם וְלֹא יִשְׁמָֽעוּ, אַף לָהֶם וְלֹא יְרִיחוּן. יְדֵיהֶם וְלֹא יְמִישׁוּן, רַגְלֵיהֶם וְלֹא יְהַלֵּֽכוּ, לֹא יֶהְגּוּ בִּגְרוֹנָם. כְּמוֹהֶם יִהְיוּ עֹשֵׂיהֶם, כֹּל אֲשֶׁר בֹּטֵֽחַ בָּהֶם. יִשְׂרָאֵל בְּטַח בַּייָ, עֶזְרָם וּמָגִנָּם הוּא. בֵּית אַהֲרֹן בִּטְחוּ בַייָ, עֶזְרָם וּמָגִנָּם הוּא. יִרְאֵי יְיָ בִּטְחוּ בַייָ, עֶזְרָם וּמָגִנָּם הוּא.

Psalm 115:12-18

יְיָ זְכָרָֽנוּ יְבָרֵךְ, יְבָרֵךְ אֶת בֵּית יִשְׂרָאֵל, יְבָרֵךְ אֶת בֵּית אַהֲרֹן. יְבָרֵךְ יִרְאֵי יְיָ, הַקְּטַנִּים עִם הַגְּדֹלִים. יֹסֵף יְיָ עֲלֵיכֶם, עֲלֵיכֶם וְעַל בְּנֵיכֶם. בְּרוּכִים אַתֶּם לַייָ, עֹשֵׂה שָׁמַֽיִם וָאָֽרֶץ. הַשָּׁמַֽיִם שָׁמַֽיִם לַייָ, וְהָאָֽרֶץ נָתַן לִבְנֵי אָדָם. לֹא הַמֵּתִים יְהַלְלוּ יָהּ, וְלֹא כָּל יֹרְדֵי דוּמָה. וַאֲנַֽחְנוּ נְבָרֵךְ יָהּ, מֵעַתָּה וְעַד עוֹלָם, הַלְלוּיָהּ.

Psalm 116:1-11

אָהַֽבְתִּי כִּי יִשְׁמַע יְיָ, אֶת קוֹלִי תַּחֲנוּנָי. כִּי הִטָּה אָזְנוֹ לִי, וּבְיָמַי אֶקְרָא. אֲפָפֽוּנִי חֶבְלֵי מָֽוֶת, וּמְצָרֵי שְׁאוֹל מְצָאֽוּנִי, צָרָה וְיָגוֹן אֶמְצָא. וּבְשֵׁם יְיָ אֶקְרָא, אָנָּה יְיָ מַלְּטָה נַפְשִׁי. חַנּוּן יְיָ וְצַדִּיק, וֵאלֹהֵֽינוּ מְרַחֵם. שֹׁמֵר פְּתָאִים יְיָ, דַּלֹּתִי וְלִי יְהוֹשִֽׁיעַ. שׁוּבִי נַפְשִׁי לִמְנוּחָֽיְכִי, כִּי יְיָ גָּמַל עָלָֽיְכִי. כִּי חִלַּֽצְתָּ נַפְשִׁי מִמָּֽוֶת, אֶת עֵינִי מִן דִּמְעָה, אֶת רַגְלִי מִדֶּֽחִי. אֶתְהַלֵּךְ לִפְנֵי יְיָ, בְּאַרְצוֹת הַחַיִּים. הֶאֱמַֽנְתִּי כִּי אֲדַבֵּר, אֲנִי עָנִֽיתִי מְאֹד. אֲנִי אָמַֽרְתִּי בְחָפְזִי, כָּל הָאָדָם כֹּזֵב.

Psalm 116:12-19

מָה אָשִׁיב לַייָ, כָּל תַּגְמוּלֽוֹהִי עָלָי. כּוֹס יְשׁוּעוֹת אֶשָּׂא, וּבְשֵׁם יְיָ אֶקְרָא. נְדָרַי לַייָ אֲשַׁלֵּם, נֶגְדָה נָּא לְכָל עַמּוֹ. יָקָר בְּעֵינֵי יְיָ, הַמָּֽוְתָה לַחֲסִידָיו. אָנָּה יְיָ כִּי אֲנִי עַבְדֶּֽךָ, אֲנִי עַבְדְּךָ בֶּן אֲמָתֶֽךָ, פִּתַּֽחְתָּ לְמוֹסֵרָי. לְךָ אֶזְבַּח זֶֽבַח תּוֹדָה, וּבְשֵׁם יְיָ אֶקְרָא. נְדָרַי לַייָ אֲשַׁלֵּם, נֶגְדָה נָּא לְכָל עַמּוֹ. בְּחַצְרוֹת בֵּית יְיָ, בְּתוֹכֵֽכִי יְרוּשָׁלָֽיִם, הַלְלוּיָהּ.

Psalm 117

הַלְלוּ אֶת יְיָ, כָּל גּוֹיִם, שַׁבְּחֽוּהוּ, כָּל הָאֻמִּים. כִּי גָבַר עָלֵֽינוּ חַסְדּוֹ, וֶאֱמֶת יְיָ לְעוֹלָם, הַלְלוּיָהּ.

Hallelu et Adonai kol goyim shab'ḥuhu, kol ha'umim. Ki gavar aleinu ḥasdo, v'emet Adonai le-olam. Halleluyah.

Hallel

Psalm 115:1-11

Not unto us, oh Lord, not unto us, but unto Thy name give glory. For Thy lovingkindness, and for Thy truth's sake. Wherefore should the nations say, where is now their God? But our God is in the heavens: He has done whatsoever He desired. Their idols are silver and gold, the work of men's hands. They have mouths, but they cannot speak, eyes but they cannot see, ears but they cannot hear, noses but they cannot smell. They have hands, but they cannot handle, feet but they cannot walk, throats but they cannot speak. They that make them shall be like them. Yes, every one that trusts in them. Oh Israel, you trust in the Lord, He is your help and shield. Oh house of Aaron, you trust in the Lord, He is your help and shield. You that fear the Lord, trust in the Lord. He is your help and shield.

Psalm 115:12-18

The Lord has been mindful of us; He will bless us. He will bless the house of Israel; He will bless the house of Aaron. He will bless them that fear the Lord, both small and great. The Lord increase you more and more, you and your children. Blessed are You, Oh Lord, who made heaven and earth. The heavens are the heavens of the Lord, but the earth has He given to the children of men. The dead do not praise the Lord, neither any that are silent, but we will bless the Lord from this time forth and for evermore. Praise the Lord!

Psalm 116:1-11

I love the Lord, because He hears my voice and my supplications. Because He has inclined His ear to me, I will call upon Him as long as I live. The cords of death compassed me, and the pains of Sheol held onto me; I found trouble and sorrow. Then I called upon the name of the Lord. Oh Lord, I beg you, deliver my soul! Gracious is the Lord, and righteous; yes, our God is merciful. The Lord preserves the simple. I was brought low, and He saved me. Return unto your rest, O my soul, for the Lord has dealt bountifully with you. For You have delivered my soul from death, my eyes from tears, and my feet from falling. I will walk before the Lord in the land of the living. I believe, for I will speak. I was greatly afflicted, and I said in my distress, all men are liars.

Psalm 116:12-19

What shall I render unto the Lord for all His benefits toward me? I will take the cup of salvation, and call upon the name of the Lord. I will pay my vows unto the Lord, yes, in the presence of all His people. Precious in the sight of the Lord is the death of His holy ones. Oh Lord, truly I am Your servant, I am Your servant, the son of Your handmaid. You have loosed my bonds. I will offer to You the sacrifice of thanksgiving, and I will call upon the name of the Lord. I will pay my vows to the Lord in the presence of all His people, in the courts of the Lord's house, in the midst of You, Oh Jerusalem. Praise the Lord!

Psalm 117

Oh praise the Lord, all you nations; Laud him, all you peoples. For His lovingkindness is great toward us, and the truth of the Lord endures forever. Praise the Lord!

Psalm 118:1-4

Reader: הוֹדוּ לַייָ כִּי טוֹב, כִּי לְעוֹלָם חַסְדּוֹ.

All: הוֹדוּ לַייָ כִּי טוֹב, כִּי לְעוֹלָם חַסְדּוֹ.

Hodu L'Adonai ki tov, Ki l'olam ḥasdo

Reader: יֹאמַר נָא יִשְׂרָאֵל, כִּי לְעוֹלָם חַסְדּוֹ.

All: הוֹדוּ לַייָ כִּי טוֹב, כִּי לְעוֹלָם חַסְדּוֹ.

Hodu L'Adonai ki tov, Ki l'olam ḥasdo

Reader: יֹאמְרוּ נָא בֵית אַהֲרֹן, כִּי לְעוֹלָם חַסְדּוֹ.

All: הוֹדוּ לַייָ כִּי טוֹב, כִּי לְעוֹלָם חַסְדּוֹ.

Hodu L'Adonai ki tov, Ki l'olam ḥasdo

Reader: יֹאמְרוּ נָא יִרְאֵי יְיָ, כִּי לְעוֹלָם חַסְדּוֹ.

All: הוֹדוּ לַייָ כִּי טוֹב, כִּי לְעוֹלָם חַסְדּוֹ.

Hodu L'Adonai ki tov, Ki l'olam ḥasdo

Psalm 118:5-29

מִן הַמֵּצַר קָרָאתִי יָּהּ, עָנָנִי בַמֶּרְחָב יָהּ. יְיָ לִי לֹא אִירָא, מַה יַּעֲשֶׂה לִי אָדָם. יְיָ לִי בְּעֹזְרָי, וַאֲנִי אֶרְאֶה בְשֹׂנְאָי. טוֹב לַחֲסוֹת בַּייָ, מִבְּטֹחַ בָּאָדָם. טוֹב לַחֲסוֹת בַּייָ, מִבְּטֹחַ בִּנְדִיבִים. כָּל גּוֹיִם סְבָבוּנִי, בְּשֵׁם יְיָ כִּי אֲמִילַם. סַבּוּנִי גַם סְבָבוּנִי, בְּשֵׁם יְיָ כִּי אֲמִילַם. סַבּוּנִי כִדְבֹרִים דֹּעֲכוּ כְּאֵשׁ קוֹצִים, בְּשֵׁם יְיָ כִּי אֲמִילַם. דָּחֹה דְחִיתַנִי לִנְפֹּל, וַייָ עֲזָרָנִי. עָזִּי וְזִמְרָת יָהּ, וַיְהִי לִי לִישׁוּעָה. קוֹל רִנָּה וִישׁוּעָה בְּאָהֳלֵי צַדִּיקִים, יְמִין יְיָ עֹשָׂה חָיִל. יְמִין יְיָ רוֹמֵמָה, יְמִין יְיָ עֹשָׂה חָיִל. לֹא אָמוּת כִּי אֶחְיֶה, וַאֲסַפֵּר מַעֲשֵׂי יָהּ. יַסֹּר יִסְּרַנִּי יָּהּ, וְלַמָּוֶת לֹא נְתָנָנִי. פִּתְחוּ לִי שַׁעֲרֵי צֶדֶק, אָבֹא בָם אוֹדֶה יָהּ. זֶה הַשַּׁעַר לַייָ, צַדִּיקִים יָבֹאוּ בוֹ.

(Each of the following verses is repeated twice)

אוֹדְךָ כִּי עֲנִיתָנִי, וַתְּהִי לִי לִישׁוּעָה.

אֶבֶן מָאֲסוּ הַבּוֹנִים, הָיְתָה לְרֹאשׁ פִּנָּה.

מֵאֵת יְיָ הָיְתָה זֹּאת, הִיא נִפְלָאת בְּעֵינֵינוּ.

זֶה הַיּוֹם עָשָׂה יְיָ, נָגִילָה וְנִשְׂמְחָה בוֹ.

Ana Adonai hoshiah na — אָנָּא יְיָ הוֹשִׁיעָה נָּא.

Ana Adonai hoshiah na — אָנָּא יְיָ הוֹשִׁיעָה נָּא.

Ana Adonai hats'liḥa na — אָנָּא יְיָ הַצְלִיחָה נָא.

Ana Adonai hats'liḥa na — אָנָּא יְיָ הַצְלִיחָה נָא.

Psalm 118:1-4

Reader : Give thanks to the Lord, for He is good; His mercy endures forever.

***All :* Give thanks to the Lord, for He is good; His mercy endures forever.**

Reader : Let Israel say; His mercy endures forever.

***All :* Give thanks to the Lord, for He is good; His mercy endures forever.**

Reader : Let the house of Aaron say; His mercy endures forever.

***All :* Give thanks to the Lord, for He is good; His mercy endures forever.**

Reader : Let those who fear the Lord say; His mercy endures forever.

***All :* Give thanks to the Lord, for He is good; His mercy endures forever.**

Psalm 118:5-29

Out of my distress I called to the Lord. The Lord answered me and set me in a good place. The Lord is on my side; I will not fear: What can man do unto me? The Lord is on my side among them that help me, therefore shall I see my success against those that hate me. It is better to take refuge in the Lord than to put confidence in man. It is better to take refuge in the Lord than to put confidence in princes. The nations surrounded me. In the name of the Lord I will cut them off. They encircled me again. In the name of the Lord I will cut them off. They surrounded me about like bees, attacking like fiery thorns. In the name of the Lord I will cut them off. They attacked heavily at me that I might fall, but the Lord helped me. The Lord is my strength and song, and He has become my salvation. The voice of rejoicing and salvation is in the tents of the righteous. The right hand of the Lord does valiantly. The right hand of the Lord is exalted. The right hand of the Lord does valiantly. I shall not die, but live and declare the works of the Lord. The Lord has disciplined me severly, but He has not given me over to death. Open to me the gates of righteousness and I will enter into them to give thanks to the Lord. This is the gate of the Lord; the righteous shall enter into it.

(Each of the following verses is repeated twice)

I will give thanks unto You for You have answered me,
and You are my salvation.
The stone which the builders rejected, is become the chief cornerstone.
This is the Lord's doing, it is marvellous in our eyes.
This is the day which the Lord has made, we will rejoice and be glad in it.

We beg Lord, please save us now!
We beg Lord, please save us now!
We beg Lord, please prosper us now!
We beg Lord, please prosper us now!

בָּרוּךְ הַבָּא בְּשֵׁם יְיָ, בֵּרַכְנוּכֶם מִבֵּית יְיָ.

אֵל יְיָ וַיָּאֶר לָנוּ, אִסְרוּ חַג בַּעֲבֹתִים עַד קַרְנוֹת הַמִּזְבֵּחַ.

אֵלִי אַתָּה וְאוֹדֶךָּ, אֱלֹהַי אֲרוֹמְמֶךָּ.

הוֹדוּ לַייָ כִּי טוֹב, כִּי לְעוֹלָם חַסְדּוֹ.

יְהַלְלוּךָ יְיָ אֱלֹהֵינוּ כָּל מַעֲשֶׂיךָ, וַחֲסִידֶיךָ צַדִּיקִים עוֹשֵׂי רְצוֹנֶךָ, וְכָל עַמְּךָ בֵּית יִשְׂרָאֵל בְּרִנָּה יוֹדוּ וִיבָרְכוּ וִישַׁבְּחוּ וִיפָאֲרוּ וִירוֹמְמוּ וְיַעֲרִיצוּ וְיַקְדִּישׁוּ וְיַמְלִיכוּ אֶת שִׁמְךָ מַלְכֵּנוּ. כִּי לְךָ טוֹב לְהוֹדוֹת וּלְשִׁמְךָ נָאֶה לְזַמֵּר, כִּי מֵעוֹלָם וְעַד עוֹלָם אַתָּה אֵל. בָּרוּךְ אַתָּה יְיָ, מֶלֶךְ מְהֻלָּל בַּתִּשְׁבָּחוֹת.

Blessed be he that comes in the name of the Lord, we have blessed you out of the House of the Lord.

The Lord is God and He has given us light, so bind the sacrifice with cords even to the horns of the altar.

You are my God and I will give You thanks, You are my God and I will exalt you.

Oh give thanks to the Lord for He is good, for His lovingkindness endures forever.

All Your works praise You, Lord our God. Your righteous followers of the House of Israel seeking to do Your will joyously thank and bless, praise and glorify, extol and honor, sanctify and proclaim Your name our King. It is good indeed to give You thanks, it is pleasant to sing praises to Your name, for You are God from eternity to eternity. Blessed are You Lord, King who is worthy of praise.

Psalm 136

הוֹדוּ לַײָ כִּי טוֹב, כִּי לְעוֹלָם חַסְדּוֹ. *Ki l'olam ḥasdo*

הוֹדוּ לֵאלֹהֵי הָאֱלֹהִים, כִּי לְעוֹלָם חַסְדּוֹ.

הוֹדוּ לַאֲדֹנֵי הָאֲדֹנִים, כִּי לְעוֹלָם חַסְדּוֹ.

לְעֹשֵׂה נִפְלָאוֹת גְּדֹלוֹת לְבַדּוֹ, כִּי לְעוֹלָם חַסְדּוֹ.

לְעֹשֵׂה הַשָּׁמַיִם בִּתְבוּנָה, כִּי לְעוֹלָם חַסְדּוֹ.

לְרוֹקַע הָאָרֶץ עַל הַמָּיִם, כִּי לְעוֹלָם חַסְדּוֹ.

לְעֹשֵׂה אוֹרִים גְּדֹלִים, כִּי לְעוֹלָם חַסְדּוֹ.

אֶת הַשֶּׁמֶשׁ לְמֶמְשֶׁלֶת בַּיּוֹם, כִּי לְעוֹלָם חַסְדּוֹ

אֶת הַיָּרֵחַ וְכוֹכָבִים לְמֶמְשְׁלוֹת בַּלָּיְלָה, כִּי לְעוֹלָם חַסְדּוֹ.

לְמַכֵּה מִצְרַיִם בִּבְכוֹרֵיהֶם, כִּי לְעוֹלָם חַסְדּוֹ.

וַיּוֹצֵא יִשְׂרָאֵל מִתּוֹכָם, כִּי לְעוֹלָם חַסְדּוֹ.

בְּיָד חֲזָקָה וּבִזְרוֹעַ נְטוּיָה, כִּי לְעוֹלָם חַסְדּוֹ.

לְגֹזֵר יַם סוּף לִגְזָרִים, כִּי לְעוֹלָם חַסְדּוֹ.

וְהֶעֱבִיר יִשְׂרָאֵל בְּתוֹכוֹ, כִּי לְעוֹלָם חַסְדּוֹ.

וְנִעֵר פַּרְעֹה וְחֵילוֹ בְיַם סוּף, כִּי לְעוֹלָם חַסְדּוֹ.

לְמוֹלִיךְ עַמּוֹ בַּמִּדְבָּר, כִּי לְעוֹלָם חַסְדּוֹ.

לְמַכֵּה מְלָכִים גְּדֹלִים, כִּי לְעוֹלָם חַסְדּוֹ.

וַיַּהֲרֹג מְלָכִים אַדִּירִים, כִּי לְעוֹלָם חַסְדּוֹ.

לְסִיחוֹן מֶלֶךְ הָאֱמֹרִי, כִּי לְעוֹלָם חַסְדּוֹ.

וּלְעוֹג מֶלֶךְ הַבָּשָׁן, כִּי לְעוֹלָם חַסְדּוֹ.

וְנָתַן אַרְצָם לְנַחֲלָה, כִּי לְעוֹלָם חַסְדּוֹ.

נַחֲלָה לְיִשְׂרָאֵל עַבְדּוֹ, כִּי לְעוֹלָם חַסְדּוֹ.

שֶׁבְּשִׁפְלֵנוּ זָכַר לָנוּ, כִּי לְעוֹלָם חַסְדּוֹ

וַיִּפְרְקֵנוּ מִצָּרֵינוּ, כִּי לְעוֹלָם חַסְדּוֹ.

נֹתֵן לֶחֶם לְכָל בָּשָׂר, כִּי לְעוֹלָם חַסְדּוֹ.

הוֹדוּ לְאֵל הַשָּׁמָיִם, כִּי לְעוֹלָם חַסְדּוֹ.

Psalm 136

Give thanks to the Lord, for He is good; His mercy endures forever.

Give thanks to the God of gods; His mercy endures forever.

Give thanks to the Lord of lords; His mercy endures forever.

To Him who alone does great things; His mercy endures forever.

To Him who made the heavens with wisdom; His mercy endures forever.

To Him who put the earth upon the waters; His mercy endures forever.

To Him who made the great lights; His mercy endures forever.

The sun to rule by day; His mercy endures forever.

The moon and the stars to rule by night; His mercy endures forever.

To Him who struck the firstborn of Egypt; His mercy endures forever.

And brought Israel from their midst; His mercy endures forever.

With a strong hand and an outstretched arm; His mercy endures forever.

To Him who divided the Red Sea; His mercy endures forever.

And made Israel pass through its midst; His mercy endures forever.

And drowned Pharaoh's army in it; His mercy endures forever.

To Him who led His people through the wilderness; His mercy endures forever.

To Him who struck down great kings; His mercy endures forever.

And slew kings of renown; His mercy endures forever.

Sihon, king of the Amorites; His mercy endures forever.

And Og, king of Bashan; His mercy endures forever.

He gave their land as an inheritance; His mercy endures forever.

An inheritance to Israel, His servant; His mercy endures forever.

Who remembered us in our low estate; His mercy endures forever.

And rescued us from our enemies; His mercy endures forever.

Who gives food to all creatures; His mercy endures forever.

Give thanks to the God of heaven; His mercy endures forever.

נִשְׁמַת כָּל חַי, תְּבָרֵךְ אֶת שִׁמְךָ יְיָ אֱלֹהֵינוּ. וְרוּחַ כָּל בָּשָׂר, תְּפָאֵר וּתְרוֹמֵם זִכְרְךָ מַלְכֵּנוּ תָּמִיד, מִן הָעוֹלָם וְעַד הָעוֹלָם אַתָּה אֵל. וּמִבַּלְעָדֶיךָ אֵין לָנוּ מֶלֶךְ גּוֹאֵל וּמוֹשִׁיעַ, פּוֹדֶה וּמַצִּיל וּמְפַרְנֵס וּמְרַחֵם, בְּכָל עֵת צָרָה וְצוּקָה. אֵין לָנוּ מֶלֶךְ אֶלָּא אָתָּה.

אֱלֹהֵי הָרִאשׁוֹנִים וְהָאַחֲרוֹנִים, אֱלוֹהַּ כָּל בְּרִיּוֹת, אֲדוֹן כָּל תּוֹלָדוֹת, הַמְהֻלָּל בְּרֹב הַתִּשְׁבָּחוֹת, הַמְנַהֵג עוֹלָמוֹ בְּחֶסֶד, וּבְרִיּוֹתָיו בְּרַחֲמִים. וַיְיָ לֹא יָנוּם וְלֹא יִישָׁן, הַמְעוֹרֵר יְשֵׁנִים וְהַמֵּקִיץ נִרְדָּמִים, וְהַמֵּשִׂיחַ אִלְּמִים, וְהַמַּתִּיר אֲסוּרִים, וְהַסּוֹמֵךְ נוֹפְלִים, וְהַזּוֹקֵף כְּפוּפִים, לְךָ לְבַדְּךָ אֲנַחְנוּ מוֹדִים.

אִלּוּ פִינוּ מָלֵא שִׁירָה כַּיָּם, וּלְשׁוֹנֵנוּ רִנָּה כַּהֲמוֹן גַּלָּיו, וְשִׂפְתוֹתֵינוּ שֶׁבַח כְּמֶרְחֲבֵי רָקִיעַ, וְעֵינֵינוּ מְאִירוֹת כַּשֶּׁמֶשׁ וְכַיָּרֵחַ, וְיָדֵינוּ פְרוּשׂוֹת כְּנִשְׁרֵי שָׁמָיִם, וְרַגְלֵינוּ קַלּוֹת כָּאַיָּלוֹת, אֵין אֲנַחְנוּ מַסְפִּיקִים, לְהוֹדוֹת לְךָ יְיָ אֱלֹהֵינוּ וֵאלֹהֵי אֲבוֹתֵינוּ, וּלְבָרֵךְ אֶת שְׁמֶךָ עַל אַחַת מֵאָלֶף אֶלֶף אַלְפֵי אֲלָפִים וְרִבֵּי רְבָבוֹת פְּעָמִים, הַטּוֹבוֹת שֶׁעָשִׂיתָ עִם אֲבוֹתֵינוּ וְעִמָּנוּ. מִמִּצְרַיִם גְּאַלְתָּנוּ יְיָ אֱלֹהֵינוּ, וּמִבֵּית עֲבָדִים פְּדִיתָנוּ. בְּרָעָב זַנְתָּנוּ, וּבְשָׂבָע כִּלְכַּלְתָּנוּ. מֵחֶרֶב הִצַּלְתָּנוּ, וּמִדֶּבֶר מִלַּטְתָּנוּ. וּמֵחֳלָיִם רָעִים וְנֶאֱמָנִים דִּלִּיתָנוּ. עַד הֵנָּה עֲזָרוּנוּ רַחֲמֶיךָ, וְלֹא עֲזָבוּנוּ חֲסָדֶיךָ וְאַל תִּטְּשֵׁנוּ. יְיָ אֱלֹהֵינוּ לָנֶצַח.

עַל כֵּן אֵבָרִים שֶׁפִּלַּגְתָּ בָּנוּ, וְרוּחַ וּנְשָׁמָה שֶׁנָּפַחְתָּ בְּאַפֵּינוּ, וְלָשׁוֹן אֲשֶׁר שַׂמְתָּ בְּפִינוּ, הֵן הֵם יוֹדוּ וִיבָרְכוּ וִישַׁבְּחוּ וִיפָאֲרוּ וִירוֹמְמוּ וְיַעֲרִיצוּ וְיַקְדִּישׁוּ וְיַמְלִיכוּ אֶת שִׁמְךָ מַלְכֵּנוּ. כִּי כָל פֶּה לְךָ יוֹדֶה, וְכָל לָשׁוֹן לְךָ תִשָּׁבַע, וְכָל בֶּרֶךְ לְךָ תִכְרַע, וְכָל קוֹמָה לְפָנֶיךָ תִשְׁתַּחֲוֶה, וְכָל לְבָבוֹת יִירָאוּךָ, וְכָל קֶרֶב וּכְלָיוֹת יְזַמְּרוּ לִשְׁמֶךָ. כַּדָּבָר שֶׁכָּתוּב, כָּל עַצְמוֹתַי תֹּאמַרְנָה יְיָ מִי כָמוֹךָ. מַצִּיל עָנִי מֵחָזָק מִמֶּנּוּ, וְעָנִי וְאֶבְיוֹן מִגֹּזְלוֹ: מִי יִדְמֶה לָּךְ, וּמִי יִשְׁוֶה לָּךְ וּמִי יַעֲרָךְ לָךְ: הָאֵל הַגָּדוֹל הַגִּבּוֹר וְהַנּוֹרָא, אֵל עֶלְיוֹן קֹנֵה שָׁמַיִם וָאָרֶץ. נְהַלֶּלְךָ וּנְשַׁבֵּחֲךָ וּנְפָאֶרְךָ וּנְבָרֵךְ אֶת־שֵׁם קָדְשֶׁךָ. כָּאָמוּר, לְדָוִד, בָּרְכִי נַפְשִׁי אֶת יְיָ, וְכָל קְרָבַי אֶת שֵׁם קָדְשׁוֹ.

הָאֵל בְּתַעֲצֻמוֹת עֻזֶּךָ, הַגָּדוֹל בִּכְבוֹד שְׁמֶךָ. הַגִּבּוֹר לָנֶצַח וְהַנּוֹרָא בְּנוֹרְאוֹתֶיךָ.

Lord our God, the soul of every living being will bless Your Name, and the spirit of all flesh will always glorify and exalt Your fame, our King. From eternity and to eternity You are God, and aside from You, we have no King who redeems and saves, ransoms and rescues, sustains and has compassion in times of trouble and distress. We have no King but You.

God of the beginning and of the end, God of all creation, Lord of all that is born; He who guides His world with loving kindness and His creation with compassion will be endlessly praised. The Lord does not slumber or sleep; it is He who wakens the sleeper and rouses the one who slumbers. He gives words to the one who is silent, and He sets the captive free. He supports those who fall and raises up those who are bowed down. To You alone we give thanks.

If our mouth was as filled with song as the sea is, and our tongue able to shout as do the waves; if our lips poured forth adoration as the heavens do, and if our eyes were as bright as the sun and moon; if our hands were outstretched as the eagles of the sky and if our feet were as swift as the deer, we would never be able to thank You for even one-thousandth of the countless millions of blessings which You bestowed on our fathers and on us. Lord, You are our God and the God of our fathers. Lord our God, You redeemed us from Egypt and brought us out of slavery. In times of famine You nourished us and satisfied us with plenty. You delivered us from the sword and made us escape the plagues. You gave us relief from severe and lasting diseases. Out of compassion You have always helped us, and in Your loving kindness You have not forsaken us. May the Lord our God never forsake us.

Therefore, the limbs which You have apportioned in us, the spirit and soul which You have breathed into our nostrils, and the tongue which You put in our mouth, shall thank and bless, praise and glorify, extol and honor, sanctify and revere Your Name, our King. Indeed, every mouth will give You praise; every tongue will swear allegiance; every person will bend the knee and bow down before You; every heart will fear You, and a person's innermost being will sing to Your Name, as it is written: "All my being will say: 'Who is like You, O Lord? You deliver the poor from one who is too strong for him, and the one who is poor and defenseless from one who would rob him.'" Who is like You? Who is equal to You? Who can be compared to You? You are the great, mighty and awesome God; the Almighty God; the Master of heaven and earth. We will praise and laud and glorify and bless Your Holy Name, as it is said by David, "May my soul bless the Lord, and my whole being honor His Holy Name."

In the power of Your might You are God; great is the honor of Your Name. You are mighty forever and You are revered for Your awesome deeds.

הַמֶּלֶךְ הַיּוֹשֵׁב עַל כִּסֵּא רָם וְנִשָּׂא!

HaMelekh hayosheiv al kisei ram v'nisa!

שׁוֹכֵן עַד, מָרוֹם וְקָדוֹשׁ שְׁמוֹ. וְכָתוּב, רַנְּנוּ צַדִּיקִים בַּיְיָ, לַיְשָׁרִים נָאוָה תְהִלָּה. בְּפִי יְשָׁרִים תִּתְהַלָּל. וּבְדִבְרֵי צַדִּיקִים תִּתְבָּרַךְ. וּבִלְשׁוֹן חֲסִידִים תִּתְרוֹמָם. וּבְקֶרֶב קְדוֹשִׁים תִּתְקַדָּשׁ.

Shokhein ahd marom v'kadosh sh'mo. V'khatuv ran'nu tsadikim, ba'Adonai la'yesharim na'va t'hillah. B'fi y'sharim tit'hallal, uv'divrei tsadikim tit'barakh. Uvil'shon ḥasidim tit'romam uv'kerev k'doshim tit'kadash.

וּבְמַקְהֲלוֹת רִבְבוֹת עַמְּךָ בֵּית יִשְׂרָאֵל, בְּרִנָּה יִתְפָּאַר שִׁמְךָ מַלְכֵּנוּ, בְּכָל דּוֹר וָדוֹר, שֶׁכֵּן חוֹבַת כָּל הַיְצוּרִים, לְפָנֶיךָ יְיָ אֱלֹהֵינוּ, וֵאלֹהֵי אֲבוֹתֵינוּ, לְהוֹדוֹת לְהַלֵּל לְשַׁבֵּחַ לְפָאֵר לְרוֹמֵם לְהַדֵּר לְבָרֵךְ לְעַלֵּה וּלְקַלֵּס, עַל כָּל דִּבְרֵי שִׁירוֹת וְתִשְׁבְּחוֹת דָּוִד בֶּן יִשַׁי עַבְדְּךָ מְשִׁיחֶךָ.

יִשְׁתַּבַּח שִׁמְךָ לָעַד מַלְכֵּנוּ, הָאֵל הַמֶּלֶךְ הַגָּדוֹל וְהַקָּדוֹשׁ בַּשָּׁמַיִם וּבָאָרֶץ. כִּי לְךָ נָאֶה, יְיָ אֱלֹהֵינוּ וֵאלֹהֵי אֲבוֹתֵינוּ, שִׁיר וּשְׁבָחָה, הַלֵּל וְזִמְרָה, עֹז וּמֶמְשָׁלָה, נֶצַח, גְּדֻלָּה וּגְבוּרָה, תְּהִלָּה וְתִפְאֶרֶת, קְדֻשָּׁה וּמַלְכוּת. בְּרָכוֹת וְהוֹדָאוֹת מֵעַתָּה וְעַד עוֹלָם. בָּרוּךְ אַתָּה יְיָ, אֵל מֶלֶךְ גָּדוֹל בַּתִּשְׁבָּחוֹת, אֵל הַהוֹדָאוֹת, אֲדוֹן הַנִּפְלָאוֹת, הַבּוֹחֵר בְּשִׁירֵי זִמְרָה, מֶלֶךְ אֵל חֵי הָעוֹלָמִים.

(Lift the Fourth Cup and say)

בָּרוּךְ אַתָּה יְיָ, אֱלֹהֵינוּ מֶלֶךְ הָעוֹלָם, בּוֹרֵא פְּרִי הַגָּפֶן.

Barukh atah Adonai Eloheinu Melekh Ha'Olam, borei p'ri ha'gafen.

(Drink the Fourth Cup reclining to the left)

The King is seated upon a high and lofty throne!

Abiding forever, His Name is exalted and holy. It is written: "Be joyful in the Lord, you righteous ones; it is fitting that the upright sing." The mouth of the upright will sing praise and by the speech of the righteous, You will be blessed. You will be extolled by the tongue of the faithful and in the midst of the holy, You will be sanctified.

In the assemblies of the tens of thousands of Your people the House of Israel, Your Name, our King, will be glorified in every generation with ringing song. This is the duty of all creatures, Lord our God, and God of our fathers, to thank, praise, laud, glorify, extol, honor, bless, exalt, and proclaim You through the words of the songs of praise of David, the son of Jesse, Your anointed servant.

Your Name will be praised forever, our King, in heaven and in earth, for You are the great and holy God and King. To You, Lord our God and God of our fathers, belong song and honor, praise and hymn, power and dominion, victory, greatness and might, renown and glory, holiness and kingship, blessings and thanks, from now and forever. Blessed are You Lord, God, King exalted through praise, God of thanksgiving, Master of wonders, who chooses songs of praise, Sovereign God of eternal life.

(Lift the Fourth Cup and say)

Blessed are You, Lord our God, King of the Universe, who creates the fruit of the vine.

(Drink the Fourth Cup reclining to the left)

The fourth cup of wine is called the Cup of Praise. This is primarily due to the fact that it is drunk following the recitation of significant portions of the Hallel (Praise) Psalms. However, that is not the only reason it is given this name. This cup is also associated with one of the promises found in Exodus 6. In verse 8, God told us that He would not only redeem us but He would also take us to be His people, and that He would be our God. What a great promise to receive! If anything, our joy at receiving this promise should inspire us to praise He who gave it. Our Messiah Yeshua told his talmidim that he would not drink this cup or the fruit of the vine again until he did so with them in the Kingdom that was, and is, to come. May we, his present day talmidim, soon behold his return in glory to restore our Jewish people and to establish his promised earthly Kingdom of Israel.

(Include words in parenthesis on Shabbat)

בָּרוּךְ אַתָּה יְיָ אֱלֹהֵינוּ מֶלֶךְ הָעוֹלָם עַל הַגֶּפֶן וְעַל פְּרִי הַגֶּפֶן. וְעַל תְּנוּבַת הַשָּׂדֶה, וְעַל אֶרֶץ חֶמְדָּה טוֹבָה וּרְחָבָה, שֶׁרָצִיתָ וְהִנְחַלְתָּ לַאֲבוֹתֵינוּ, לֶאֱכוֹל מִפִּרְיָהּ וְלִשְׂבּוֹעַ מִטּוּבָהּ. רַחֵם נָא יְיָ אֱלֹהֵינוּ עַל יִשְׂרָאֵל עַמֶּךָ, וְעַל יְרוּשָׁלַיִם עִירֶךָ, וְעַל צִיּוֹן מִשְׁכַּן כְּבוֹדֶךָ, וְעַל מִזְבְּחֶךָ וְעַל הֵיכָלֶךָ.

וּבְנֵה יְרוּשָׁלַיִם עִיר הַקֹּדֶשׁ בִּמְהֵרָה בְיָמֵינוּ, וְהַעֲלֵנוּ לְתוֹכָהּ, וְשַׂמְּחֵנוּ בְּבִנְיָנָהּ וְנֹאכַל מִפִּרְיָהּ וְנִשְׂבַּע מִטּוּבָהּ, וּנְבָרֶכְךָ עָלֶיהָ בִּקְדֻשָּׁה וּבְטָהֳרָה. (וּרְצֵה וְהַחֲלִיצֵנוּ בְּיוֹם הַשַּׁבָּת הַזֶּה) וְשַׂמְּחֵנוּ בְּיוֹם חַג הַמַּצּוֹת הַזֶּה. כִּי אַתָּה יְיָ טוֹב וּמֵטִיב לַכֹּל, וְנוֹדֶה לְּךָ עַל הָאָרֶץ וְעַל פְּרִי הַגָּפֶן. בָּרוּךְ אַתָּה יְיָ, עַל הָאָרֶץ וְעַל פְּרִי הַגָּפֶן.

נרצה

חֲסַל סִדּוּר פֶּסַח כְּהִלְכָתוֹ, כְּכָל מִשְׁפָּטוֹ וְחֻקָּתוֹ. כַּאֲשֶׁר זָכִינוּ לְסַדֵּר אוֹתוֹ, כֵּן נִזְכֶּה לַעֲשׂוֹתוֹ. זָךְ שׁוֹכֵן מְעוֹנָה, קוֹמֵם קְהַל עֲדַת מִי מָנָה. בְּקָרוֹב נַהֵל נִטְעֵי כַנָּה, פְּדוּיִם לְצִיּוֹן בְּרִנָּה.

לְשָׁנָה הַבָּאָה בִּירוּשָׁלָיִם!

L'shanah haba'ah birushalayim!

בּוֹא נָא אָדוֹן יֵשׁוּעַ הַמָּשִׁיחַ בִּמְהֵרָה בְיָמֵינוּ!

Bo nah Adon Yeishua HaMashiaḥ bimherah b'yameinu!

(If this is a second night Seder, continue by beginning the omer count on the next page)

(Include the words in parenthesis on Shabbat)
Blessed are You, Lord our God, King of the Universe, for the vine and for its fruit, and for the produce of the good and spacious land which You gave as an inheritance to our fathers, that they might eat of its fruit and enjoy its goodness. Lord our God, have compassion on Israel Your people, and on Jerusalem Your city, and on Tsiyon the dwelling place of Your glory, and on Your altar and Your Temple.

May You restore Jerusalem, the Holy City, soon; even in our days. Fill us with joy by bringing the time of its restoration, that we might eat of its fruit and enjoy its goodness. We will bless You for its restoration to holiness and purity. ***(Favor us and strengthen us on this Shabbat day and)*** Make us joyful on this Festival of Matsah. Lord, You are good; You are good to all. Again, we thank You for the land and for fruit from the vine. Blessed are You, Lord, for the land and for fruit from the vine.

Nir'tsah

In accord with customs, statutes, and ordinances this Seder is now ended. As we have been privileged to celebrate this Seder now, may we be privileged to celebrate it in the future. Pure One who dwells in the highest heights, speedily restore the prosperity of Tsiyon.

NEXT YEAR IN JERUSALEM!

***Come Lord Messiah Yeshua,
speedily in our Days!***

(If this is a second night Seder, continue by beginning the omer count on the next page)

Blessing for the Counting of the Omer

(Recite this blessing after sundown at the conclusion of the second night Passover Seder on the 16th of Nisan)

בָּרוּךְ אַתָּה יְיָ אֱלֹהֵינוּ מֶלֶךְ הָעוֹלָם, אֲשֶׁר קִדְּשָׁנוּ בְּמִצְוֹתָיו, וְצִוָּנוּ עַל סְפִירַת הָעוֹמֶר.

Barukh atah Adonai, Eloheinu Melekh Ha'Olam, asher kid'shanu b'mitsvotav v'tsivanu al sefirat haomer.

Blessed are You, Lord our God, King of the Universe who sanctifies us by His commandments and who has commanded us to count the omer.

Today is day one of the omer count.

Dayenu!

Ilu ho-tsi, ho-tsi-a-nu, Ho-tsi-a-nu mi-Mitz-ra-yim,
Ho-tsi-a-nu mi-Mitz-ra-yim, Da-ye-nu!

CHORUS

Dai, da-ye-nu, Dai, da-ye-nu,
Dai, da-ye-nu, Da-ye-nu, da-ye-nu, da-ye-nu!
(Repeat Twice)

Ilu na-tan, na-tan la-nu, Na-tan la-nu et-ha-Sha-bat,
Na-tan la-nu et-ha-Sha-bat, Da-ye-nu!

(Return to Chorus)

Ilu na-tan, na-tan la-nu, Na-tan la-nu et-ha-To-rah,
Na-tan la-nu et-ha-To-rah, Da-ye-nu!

(Return to Chorus)

Ilu na-tan, na-tan la-nu, Na-tan la-nu et-Ye-shu-a,
Na-tan la-nu et- Ye-shu-a, Da-ye-nu!

(Return to Chorus)

Had He only taken us out of Egypt: it would have been enough for us!
Had He only given us the Shabbat: it would have been enough for us!
Had He only given us the Torah: it would have been enough for us!
Had He only given us Salvation: it would have been enough for us!

אדיר הוא

אַדִּיר הוּא יִבְנֶה בֵּיתוֹ בְּקָרוֹב.
בִּמְהֵרָה, בִּמְהֵרָה, בְּיָמֵינוּ בְּקָרוֹב.
אֵל בְּנֵה, אֵל בְּנֵה, בְּנֵה בֵּיתְךָ בְּקָרוֹב.

בָּחוּר הוּא, גָּדוֹל הוּא, דָּגוּל הוּא יִבְנֶה בֵּיתוֹ בְּקָרוֹב.
בִּמְהֵרָה, בִּמְהֵרָה, בְּיָמֵינוּ בְּקָרוֹב.
אֵל בְּנֵה, אֵל בְּנֵה, בְּנֵה בֵּיתְךָ בְּקָרוֹב.

הָדוּר הוּא, וָתִיק הוּא, זַכַּאי הוּא יִבְנֶה בֵּיתוֹ בְּקָרוֹב.
בִּמְהֵרָה, בִּמְהֵרָה, בְּיָמֵינוּ בְּקָרוֹב.
אֵל בְּנֵה, אֵל בְּנֵה, בְּנֵה בֵּיתְךָ בְּקָרוֹב.

חָסִיד הוּא, טָהוֹר הוּא, יָחִיד הוּא יִבְנֶה בֵּיתוֹ בְּקָרוֹב.
בִּמְהֵרָה, בִּמְהֵרָה, בְּיָמֵינוּ בְּקָרוֹב.
אֵל בְּנֵה, אֵל בְּנֵה, בְּנֵה בֵּיתְךָ בְּקָרוֹב.

כַּבִּיר הוּא, לָמוּד הוּא, מֶלֶךְ הוּא יִבְנֶה בֵּיתוֹ בְּקָרוֹב.
בִּמְהֵרָה, בִּמְהֵרָה, בְּיָמֵינוּ בְּקָרוֹב.
אֵל בְּנֵה, אֵל בְּנֵה, בְּנֵה בֵּיתְךָ בְּקָרוֹב.

נוֹרָא הוּא, סַגִּיב הוּא, עִזּוּז הוּא יִבְנֶה בֵּיתוֹ בְּקָרוֹב.
בִּמְהֵרָה, בִּמְהֵרָה, בְּיָמֵינוּ בְּקָרוֹב.
אֵל בְּנֵה, אֵל בְּנֵה, בְּנֵה בֵּיתְךָ בְּקָרוֹב.

פּוֹדֶה הוּא, צַדִּיק הוּא, קָדוֹשׁ הוּא יִבְנֶה בֵּיתוֹ בְּקָרוֹב.
בִּמְהֵרָה, בִּמְהֵרָה, בְּיָמֵינוּ בְּקָרוֹב.
אֵל בְּנֵה, אֵל בְּנֵה, בְּנֵה בֵּיתְךָ בְּקָרוֹב.

רַחוּם הוּא, שַׁדַּי הוּא, תַּקִּיף הוּא יִבְנֶה בֵּיתוֹ בְּקָרוֹב.
בִּמְהֵרָה, בִּמְהֵרָה, בְּיָמֵינוּ בְּקָרוֹב.
אֵל בְּנֵה, אֵל בְּנֵה, בְּנֵה בֵּיתְךָ בְּקָרוֹב.

Adir Hu

Adir hu yiv'neh bei-to b'karov.
Bim'hei-rah, bim'hei-rah, b'yamei-nu b'karov.
Eil b'neih, eil b'neih, b'neih beit'kha b'karov.

Baḥur hu, gadol hu, dagul hu yiv'neh bei-to b'karov.
Bim'hei-rah, bim'hei-rah, b'yamei-nu b'karov.
Eil b'neih, eil b'neih, b'neih beit'kha b'karov.

Hadur hu, vatik hu, zakhay hu yiv'neh bei-to b'karov.
Bim'hei-rah, bim'hei-rah, b'yamei-nu b'karov.
Eil b'neih, eil b'neih, b'neih beit'kha b'karov.

Ḥasid hu, tahor hu, yaḥid hu yiv'neh bei-to b'karov.
Bim'hei-rah, bim'hei-rah, b'yamei-nu b'karov.
Eil b'neih, eil b'neih, b'neih beit'kha b'karov.

Kabir hu, lamud hu, melekh hu yiv'neh bei-to b'karov.
Bim'hei-rah, bim'hei-rah, b'yamei-nu b'karov.
Eil b'neih, eil b'neih, b'neih beit'kha b'karov.

Norah hu, sagiv hu, izuz hu yiv'neh bei-to b'karov.
Bim'hei-rah, bim'hei-rah, b'yamei-nu b'karov.
Eil b'neih, eil b'neih, b'neih beit'kha b'karov.

Podeh hu, tsaddik hu, kadosh hu yiv'neh bei-to b'karov.
Bim'hei-rah, bim'hei-rah, b'yamei-nu b'karov.
Eil b'neih, eil b'neih, b'neih beit'kha b'karov.

Raḥum hu, shaddai hu, takif hu yiv'neh bei-to b'karov.
Bim'hei-rah, bim'hei-rah, b'yamei-nu b'karov.
Eil b'neih, eil b'neih, b'neih beit'kha b'karov.

May God build the Temple soon, speedily in our time, soon. God - build; God - build, build your House soon! Supreme is God, Great is God, Outstanding is God (chorus). Glorious is God, Faithful is God, Worthy is God (chorus). Kind is God, Pure is God, Unique is God (chorus). Mighty is God, Wise is God, Majestic is God (chorus). Awesome is God, Strong is God, Powerful is God (chorus). Redeeming is God, Righteous is God, Holy is God (chorus). Compassionate is God, Almighty is God, Resolute is God, May God build the Temple soon, Speedily in our time, soon. God - build; God - build, Build your House soon!

אחד מי יודע

אֶחָד מִי יוֹדֵעַ?

אֶחָד אֲנִי יוֹדֵעַ: אֶחָד אֱלֹהֵינוּ שֶׁבַּשָּׁמַיִם וּבָאָרֶץ.

שְׁנַיִם מִי יוֹדֵעַ?

שְׁנַיִם אֲנִי יוֹדֵעַ: שְׁנֵי לֻחוֹת הַבְּרִית. אֶחָד אֱלֹהֵינוּ שֶׁבַּשָּׁמַיִם וּבָאָרֶץ.

שְׁלֹשָׁה מִי יוֹדֵעַ?

שְׁלֹשָׁה אֲנִי יוֹדֵעַ: שְׁלֹשָׁה אָבוֹת, שְׁנֵי לֻחוֹת הַבְּרִית. אֶחָד אֱלֹהֵינוּ שֶׁבַּשָּׁמַיִם וּבָאָרֶץ.

אַרְבַּע מִי יוֹדֵעַ?

אַרְבַּע אֲנִי יוֹדֵעַ: אַרְבַּע אִמָּהוֹת, שְׁלֹשָׁה אָבוֹת, שְׁנֵי לֻחוֹת הַבְּרִית. אֶחָד אֱלֹהֵינוּ שֶׁבַּשָּׁמַיִם וּבָאָרֶץ.

חֲמִשָּׁה מִי יוֹדֵעַ?

חֲמִשָּׁה אֲנִי יוֹדֵעַ: חֲמִשָּׁה חוּמְשֵׁי תוֹרָה, אַרְבַּע אִמָּהוֹת, שְׁלֹשָׁה אָבוֹת, שְׁנֵי לֻחוֹת הַבְּרִית. אֶחָד אֱלֹהֵינוּ שֶׁבַּשָּׁמַיִם וּבָאָרֶץ.

שִׁשָּׁה מִי יוֹדֵעַ?

שִׁשָּׁה אֲנִי יוֹדֵעַ: שִׁשָּׁה סִדְרֵי מִשְׁנָה, חֲמִשָּׁה חוּמְשֵׁי תוֹרָה, אַרְבַּע אִמָּהוֹת, שְׁלֹשָׁה אָבוֹת, שְׁנֵי לֻחוֹת הַבְּרִית. אֶחָד אֱלֹהֵינוּ שֶׁבַּשָּׁמַיִם וּבָאָרֶץ.

שִׁבְעָה מִי יוֹדֵעַ?

שִׁבְעָה אֲנִי יוֹדֵעַ: שִׁבְעָה יְמֵי שַׁבַּתָּא, שִׁשָּׁה סִדְרֵי מִשְׁנָה, חֲמִשָּׁה חוּמְשֵׁי תוֹרָה, אַרְבַּע אִמָּהוֹת, שְׁלֹשָׁה אָבוֹת, שְׁנֵי לֻחוֹת הַבְּרִית אֶחָד אֱלֹהֵינוּ שֶׁבַּשָּׁמַיִם וּבָאָרֶץ.

שְׁמוֹנָה מִי יוֹדֵעַ?

שְׁמוֹנָה אֲנִי יוֹדֵעַ: שְׁמוֹנָה יְמֵי מִילָה, שִׁבְעָה יְמֵי שַׁבַּתָּא, שִׁשָּׁה סִדְרֵי מִשְׁנָה, חֲמִשָּׁה חוּמְשֵׁי תוֹרָה, אַרְבַּע אִמָּהוֹת, שְׁלֹשָׁה אָבוֹת, שְׁנֵי לֻחוֹת הַבְּרִית, אֶחָד אֱלֹהֵינוּ שֶׁבַּשָּׁמַיִם וּבָאָרֶץ.

תִּשְׁעָה מִי יוֹדֵעַ?

תִּשְׁעָה אֲנִי יוֹדֵעַ: תִּשְׁעָה יַרְחֵי לֵדָה, שְׁמוֹנָה יְמֵי מִילָה, שִׁבְעָה יְמֵי שַׁבַּתָּא, שִׁשָּׁה סִדְרֵי מִשְׁנָה, חֲמִשָּׁה חוּמְשֵׁי תוֹרָה, אַרְבַּע אִמָּהוֹת, שְׁלֹשָׁה אָהַבוֹת, שְׁנֵי לֻחוֹת הַבְּרִית, אֶחָד אֱלֹהֵינוּ שֶׁבַּשָּׁמַיִם וּבָאָרֶץ.

עֲשָׂרָה מִי יוֹדֵעַ?

עֲשָׂרָה אֲנִי יוֹדֵעַ: עֲשָׂרָה דִבְּרַיָּא, תִּשְׁעָה יַרְחֵי לֵדָה, שְׁמוֹנָה יְמֵי מִילָה, שִׁבְעָה יְמֵי שַׁבַּתָּא, שִׁשָּׁה סִדְרֵי מִשְׁנָה, חֲמִשָּׁה חוּמְשֵׁי תוֹרָה, אַרְבַּעאִ מָּהוֹת, שְׁלֹשָׁה אָהַבוֹת, שְׁנֵי לֻחוֹת הַבְּרִית, אֶחָד אֱלֹהֵינוּ שֶׁבַּשָּׁמַיִם וּבָאָרֶץ.

אַחַד עָשָׂר מִי יוֹדֵעַ?

אַחַד עָשָׂר אֲנִי יוֹדֵעַ: אַחַד עָשָׂר כּוֹכְבַיָּא, עֲשָׂרָה דִבְּרַיָּא, תִּשְׁעָה יַרְחֵי לֵדָה, שְׁמוֹנָה יְמֵי מִילָה, שִׁבְעָה יְמֵי שַׁבַּתָּא, שִׁשָּׁה סִדְרֵי מִשְׁנָה, חֲמִשָּׁה חוּמְשֵׁי תוֹרָה, אַרְבַּעאִ מָּהוֹת, שְׁלֹשָׁה אָהַבוֹת, שְׁנֵי לֻחוֹת הַבְּרִית, אֶחָד אֱלֹהֵינוּ שֶׁבַּשָּׁמַיִם וּבָאָרֶץ.

שְׁנֵים עָשָׂר מִי יוֹדֵעַ?

שְׁנֵים עָשָׂר אֲנִי יוֹדֵעַ: שְׁנֵים עָשָׂר שִׁבְטַיָּא, אַחַד עָשָׂר כּוֹכְבַיָּא, עֲשָׂרָה דִבְּרַיָּא, תִּשְׁעָה יַרְחֵי לֵדָה, שְׁמוֹנָה יְמֵי מִילָה, שִׁבְעָה יְמֵי שַׁבַּתָּא, שִׁשָּׁה סִדְרֵי מִשְׁנָה, חֲמִשָּׁה חוּמְשֵׁי תוֹרָה, אַרְבַּעאִ מָּהוֹת, שְׁלֹשָׁה אָהַבוֹת, שְׁנֵי לֻחוֹת הַבְּרִית, אֶחָד אֱלֹהֵינוּ שֶׁבַּשָּׁמַיִם וּבָאָרֶץ.

שְׁלֹשָׁה עָשָׂר מִי יוֹדֵעַ?

שְׁלֹשָׁה עָשָׂר אֲנִי יוֹדֵעַ: שְׁלֹשָׁה עָשָׂר מִדַּיָּא, שְׁנֵים עָשָׂר שִׁבְטַיָּא, אַחַד עָשָׂר כּוֹכְבַיָּא, עֲשָׂרָה דִבְּרַיָּא, תִּשְׁעָה יַרְחֵי לֵדָה, שְׁמוֹנָה יְמֵי מִילָה, שִׁבְעָה יְמֵי שַׁבַּתָּא, שִׁשָּׁה סִדְרֵי מִשְׁנָה, חֲמִשָּׁה חוּמְשֵׁי תוֹרָה, אַרְבַּעאִ מָּהוֹת, שְׁלֹשָׁה אָהַבוֹת, שְׁנֵי לֻחוֹת הַבְּרִית, אֶחָד אֱלֹהֵינוּ שֶׁבַּשָּׁמַיִם וּבָאָרֶץ.

Eḥad Mi Yodeah?

Eḥad mi yodei-ah?
Eḥad mi yodei-ah: Eḥad Eloheinu shebashamayim u-va'aretz.

Sh'nayim mi yodei-ah?
Sh'nayim ani yodei-ah: sh'nei luḥot hab'rit, eḥad Eloheinu shebashamayim u-va'aretz.

Sh'loshah mi yodei-ah?
Sh'loshah ani yodei-ah: sh'loshah avot, sh'nei luḥot hab'rit, eḥad Eloheinu shebashamayim u-va'aretz.

Arbah mi yodei-ah?
Arbah ani yodei-ah: arbah imahot, sh'loshah avot, sh'nei luḥot hab'rit, eḥad Eloheinu shebashamayim u-va'aretz.

Ḥamishah mi yodei-ah?
Ḥamishah ani yodei-ah: ḥamishah ḥum'she Torah, arbah imahot, sh'loshah avot, sh'nei luḥot hab'rit, eḥad Eloheinu shebashamayim u-va'aretz.

Shisha mi yodei-ah?
Shisha ani yodei-ah: shishah sid'rei mish'nah, ḥamishah ḥum'she Torah, arbah imahot, sh'loshah avot, sh'nei luḥot hab'rit, eḥad Eloheinu shebashamayim u-va'aretz.

Shiv'ah mi yodei-ah?
Shiv'ah ani yodei-ah: shiv'ah y'mei shabata, shishah sid'rei mish'nah, ḥamishah ḥum'she Torah, arbah imahot, sh'loshah avot, sh'nei luḥot hab'rit, eḥad Eloheinu shebashamayim u-va'aretz.

Sh'monah mi yodei-ah?
Sh'monah ani yodei-ah: sh'monah y'mei milah, shiv'ah y'mei shabata, shishah sid'rei mish'nah, ḥamishah ḥum'she Torah, arbah imahot, sh'loshah avot, sh'nei luḥot hab'rit, eḥad Eloheinu shebashamayim u-va'aretz.

Tish'ah mi yodei-ah?
Tish'ah ani yodei-ah: tish'ah yar'ḥei lei-dah, sh'monah y'mei milah, shiv'ah y'mei shabata, shishah sid'rei mish'nah, ḥamishah ḥum'she Torah, arbah imahot, sh'loshah avot, sh'nei luḥot hab'rit, eḥad Eloheinu shebashamayim u-va'aretz.

Asarah mi yode-ah?
Asarah ani yode-ah: asarah dib'raya, tish'ah yar'ḥei lei-dah, sh'monah y'mei milah, shiv'ah y'mei shabata, shishah sid'rei mish'nah, ḥamishah ḥum'she Torah, arbah imahot, sh'loshah avot, sh'nei luḥot hab'rit, eḥad Eloheinu shebashamayim u-va'aretz.

Aḥad asar mi yodei-ah?
Aḥad asar ani yodei-ah: aḥad asar cokh'vaya, asarah dib'raya, tish'ah yar'ḥei lei-dah, sh'monah y'mei milah, shiv'ah y'mei shabata, shishah sid'rei mish'nah, ḥamishah ḥum'she Torah, arbah imahot, sh'loshah avot, sh'nei luḥot hab'rit, eḥad Eloheinu shebashamayim u-va'aretz.

Sh'neim asar mi yodei-ah?
Sh'neim asar mi yodei-ah: sh'neim asar shiv'taya, aḥad asar cokh'vaya, asarah dib'raya, tish'ah yar'ḥei lei-dah, sh'monah y'mei milah, shiv'ah y'mei shabata, shishah sid'rei mish'nah, ḥamishah ḥum'she Torah, arbah imahot, sh'loshah avot, sh'nei luḥot hab'rit, eḥad Eloheinu shebashamayim u-va'aretz.

Sh'loshah asar mi yodei-ah?
Sh'loshah asar mi yodei-ah: sh'loshah asar mi-daya. sh'neim asar shiv'taya, aḥad asar cokh'vaya, asarah dib'raya, tish'ah yar'ḥei lei-dah, sh'monah y'mei milah, shiv'ah y'mei shabata, shishah sid'rei mish'nah, ḥamishah ḥum'she Torah, arbah imahot, sh'loshah avot, sh'nei luḥot hab'rit, eḥad Eloheinu shebashamayim u-va'aretz.

Eḥad Mi Yodeah?

Who knows One?
I know one: One is our God in the heavens and the earth.

Who knows Two?
I know two: two are the Tablets of the Covenant, One is our God in the heavens and the earth.

Who knows Three?
I know three: three are the Fathers, two are the Tablets of the Covenant, One is our God in the heavens and the earth.

Who knows Four?
I know four: four are the Mothers, three are the Fathers, two are the Tablets of the Covenant, One is our God in the heavens and the earth.

Who knows Five?
I know five: five are the books of the Torah, four are the Mothers, three are the Fathers, two are the Tablets of the Covenant, One is our God in the heavens and the earth.

Who knows Six?
I know six: six are the orders of the Mishnah, five are the books of the Torah, four are the Mothers, three are the Fathers, two are the Tablets of the Covenant, One is our God in the heavens and the earth.

Who knows Seven?
I know seven: seven are the days of the week, six are the orders of the Mishnah, five are the books of the Torah, four are the Mothers, three are the Fathers, two are the Tablets of the Covenant, One is our God in the heavens and the earth.

Who knows Eight?
I know eight: eight are the days of circumcision, seven are the days of the week, six are the orders of the Mishnah, five are the books of the Torah, four are the Mothers, three are the Fathers, two are the Tablets of the Covenant, One is our God in the heavens and the earth.

Who knows Nine?
I know nine: nine are the months of birth, eight are the days of circumcision, seven are the days of the week, six are the orders of the Mishnah, five are the books of the Torah, four are the Mothers, three are the Fathers, two are the Tablets of the Covenant, One is our God in the heavens and the earth.

Who knows Ten?
I know ten: ten are the Statements, nine are the months of birth, eight are the days of circumcision, seven are the days of the week, six are the orders of the Mishnah, five are the books of the Torah, four are the Mothers, three are the Fathers, two are the Tablets of the Covenant, One is our God in the heavens and the earth.

Who knows Eleven?
I know eleven: eleven are the stars, ten are the Statements, nine are the months of birth, eight are the days of circumcision, seven are the days of the week, six are the orders of the Mishnah, five are the books of the Torah, four are the Mothers, three are the Fathers, two are the Tablets of the Covenant, One is our God in the heavens and the earth.

Who knows Twelve?
I know twelve: twelve are the Tribes, eleven are the stars, ten are the Statements, nine are the months of birth, eight are the days of circumcision, seven are the days of the week, six are the orders of the Mishnah, five are the books of the Torah, four are the Mothers, three are the Fathers, two are the Tablets of the Covenant, One is our God in the heavens and the earth.

Who knows Thirteen?
I know thirteen: thirteen are the Characteristics, twelve are the Tribes, eleven are the stars, ten are the Statements, nine are the months of birth, eight are the days of circumcision, seven are the days of the week, six are the orders of the Mishnah, five are the books of the Torah, four are the Mothers, three are the Fathers, two are the Tablets of the Covenant, One is our God in the heavens and the earth.

חַד גַּדְיָא

חַד גַּדְיָא, חַד גַּדְיָא
דְּזַבִּין אַבָּא בִּתְרֵי זוּזֵי, חַד גַּדְיָא, חַד גַּדְיָא.

וְאָתָא שׁוּנְרָא וְאָכְלָה לְגַדְיָא, דְּזַבִּין אַבָּא בִּתְרֵי זוּזֵי, חַד גַּדְיָא, חַד גַּדְיָא.

וְאָתָא כַּלְבָּא וְנָשַׁךְ לְשׁוּנְרָא, דְּאָכְלָה לְגַדְיָא. דְּזַבִּין אַבָּא בִּתְרֵי זוּזֵי, חַד גַּדְיָא, חַד גַּדְיָא.

וְאָתָא חוּטְרָא וְהִכָּה לְכַלְבָּא, דְּנָשַׁךְ לְשׁוּנְרָא, דְּאָכְלָה לְגַדְיָא.
דְּזַבִּין אַבָּא בִּתְרֵי זוּזֵי, חַד גַּדְיָא, חַד גַּדְיָא.

וְאָתָא נוּרָא וְשָׂרַף לְחוּטְרָא, דְּהִכָּה לְכַלְבָּא, דְּנָשַׁךְ לְשׁוּנְרָא,
דְּאָכְלָה לְגַדְיָא. דְּזַבִּין אַבָּא בִּתְרֵי זוּזֵי, חַד גַּדְיָא, חַד גַּדְיָא.

וְאָתָא מַיָּא וְכָבָה לְנוּרָא, דְּשָׂרַף לְחוּטְרָא, דְּהִכָּה לְכַלְבָּא, דְּנָשַׁךְ לְשׁוּנְרָא, דְּאָכְלָה לְגַדְיָא. דְּזַבִּין אַבָּא בִּתְרֵי זוּזֵי, חַד גַּדְיָא, חַד גַּדְיָא.

וְאָתָא תוֹרָא וְשָׁתָה לְמַיָּא, דְּכָבָה לְנוּרָא, דְּשָׂרַף לְחוּטְרָא, דְּהִכָּה לְכַלְבָּא, דְּנָשַׁךְ לְשׁוּנְרָא, דְּאָכְלָה לְגַדְיָא. דְּזַבִּין אַבָּא בִּתְרֵי זוּזֵי,
חַד גַּדְיָא, חַד גַּדְיָא.

וְאָתָא הַשּׁוֹחֵט וְשָׁחַט לְתוֹרָא, דְּשָׁתָה לְמַיָּא, דְּכָבָה לְנוּרָא, דְּשָׂרַף לְחוּטְרָא, דְּהִכָּה לְכַלְבָּא, דְּנָשַׁךְ לְשׁוּנְרָא, דְּאָכְלָה לְגַדְיָא. דְּזַבִּין אַבָּא בִּתְרֵי זוּזֵי, חַד גַּדְיָא, חַד גַּדְיָא.

וְאָתָא מַלְאַךְ הַמָּוֶת וְשָׁחַט לְשׁוֹחֵט, דְּשָׁחַט לְתוֹרָא, דְּשָׁתָה לְמַיָּא,
דְּכָבָה לְנוּרָא, דְּשָׂרַף לְחוּטְרָא, דְּהִכָּה לְכַלְבָּא, דְּנָשַׁךְ לְשׁוּנְרָא,
דְּאָכְלָה לְגַדְיָא. דְּזַבִּין אַבָּא בִּתְרֵי זוּזֵי, חַד גַּדְיָא, חַד גַּדְיָא.

וְאָתָא הַקָּדוֹשׁ בָּרוּךְ הוּא וְשָׁחַט לְמַלְאַךְ הַמָּוֶת, דְּשָׁחַט לְשׁוֹחֵט,
דְּשָׁחַט לְתוֹרָא, דְּשָׁתָה לְמַיָּא, דְּכָבָה לְנוּרָא, דְּשָׂרַף לְחוּטְרָא,
דְּהִכָּה לְכַלְבָּא, דְּנָשַׁךְ לְשׁוּנְרָא, דְּאָכְלָה לְגַדְיָא.
דְּזַבִּין אַבָּא בִּתְרֵי זוּזֵי, חַד גַּדְיָא, חַד גַּדְיָא.

Ḥad Gadya

Ḥad gadya, ḥad gadya.
Dezabin aba bitrei zuzei, ḥad gadya, ḥad gadya.

V'ata shun'ra v'akhla l'gadya, d'zabin aba bit'rei zuzei, ḥad gadya, ḥad gadya

V'ata kal'ba v'nashakh l'shun-ra, d'akh-lah l'gad'ya. D'zabin aba bit'rei zuzei, ḥad gadya, ḥad gadya.

V'ata ḥutra v'hika l'khal-ba, d'nashakh l'shun'ra, d'akh-lah l'gad'ya. D'zabin aba bit'rei zuzei, ḥad gadya, ḥad gadya.

V'ata nura v'saraf l'ḥutra, d'hika l'khal-ba, d'nashakh l'shun'ra, d'akh-lah l'gad'ya. D'zabin aba bit'rei zuzei, ḥad gadya, ḥad gadya.

V'ata maya v'khava l'nura, d'saraf l'ḥut-ra, d'hika l'khal-ba, d'nashakh l'shun'ra, d'akh-lah l'gad'ya. D'zabin aba bit'rei zuzei, ḥad gadya, ḥad gadya.

V'ata tora v'shata l'maya, d'khavah l'nura, d'saraf l'ḥut-ra, d'hika l'khal-ba, d'nashakh l'shun'ra, d'akh-lah l'gad'ya. D'zabin aba bit'rei zuzei, ḥad gadya, ḥad gadya.

V'ata hashoḥet v'shaḥat l'tora, d'shatah l'maya, d'khavah l'nura, d'saraf l'ḥut-ra, d'hika l'khal-ba, d'nashakh l'shun'ra, d'akh-lah l'gad'ya. D'zabin aba bit'rei zuzei, ḥad gadya, ḥad gadya.

V'ata malakh hamavet v'shaḥat l'shoḥet, d'shaḥat l'tora, d'shatah l'maya, d'khavah l'nura, d'saraf l'ḥut-ra, d'hika l'khal-ba, d'nashakh l'shun'ra, d'akh-lah l'gad'ya. D'zabin aba bit'rei zuzei, ḥad gadya, ḥad gadya.

V'ata haKodosh barukh hu, v'shaḥat l'malakh ha-mavet, d'shaḥat l'shoḥeit, d'shaḥat l'tora, d'shatah l'maya, d'khavah l'nura, d'saraf l'ḥut-ra, d'hika l'khal-ba, d'nashakh l'shun'ra, d'akh-lah l'gad'ya. D'zabin aba bit'rei zuzei, ḥad gadya, ḥad gadya.

Ḥad Gadya

Ḥad gadya, ḥad gadya.

That father bought for two zuzim, ḥad gadya, ḥad gadya.

Then came a cat and ate the goat, that father bought for two zuzim, ḥad gadya, ḥad gadya.

Then came a dog and bit the cat, that ate the goat, that father bought for two zuzim, ḥad gadya, ḥad gadya.

Then came a stick and beat the dog, that bit the cat, that ate the goat, that father bought for two zuzim, ḥad gadya, ḥad gadya.

Then came fire and burnt the stick, that beat the dog, that bit the cat, that ate the goat, that father bought for two zuzim, ḥad gadya, ḥad gadya.

Then came water and quenched the fire, that burnt the stick, that beat the dog, that bit the cat, that ate the goat, that father bought for two zuzim, ḥad gadya, ḥad gadya.

Then came an ox and drank the water, that quenched the fire, that burnt the stick, that beat the dog, that bit the cat, that ate the goat, that father bought for two zuzim, ḥad gadya, ḥad gadya.

Then came a butcher and slaughtered the ox, that drank the water, that quenched the fire, that burnt the stick, that beat the dog, that bit the cat, that ate the goat, that father bought for two zuzim, ḥad gadya, ḥad gadya.

Then came the Angel of Death and killed the butcher, that slaughtered the ox, that drank the water, that quenched the fire, that burnt the stick, that beat the dog, that bit the cat, that ate the goat, that father bought for two zuzim, ḥad gadya, ḥad gadya.

Then came the Holy One, Blessed be He and slew the the Angel of Death, that killed the butcher, that slaughtered the ox, that drank the water, that quenched the fire, that burnt the stick, that beat the dog, that bit the cat, that ate the goat, that father bought for two zuzim, ḥad gadya, ḥad gadya.

Bibliography

Bokser, Baruch M.
'The Origins of the Seder - The Passover Rite and Early Judaism'
(University of California Press, Berkeley, Los Angeles, 1984)
Pages 50-62, 14-28

Daube, David
'He that Cometh'
(Council for Christian-Jewish Understanding, London, 1966)

Garber, Zev & Kenneth Hanson
'The Annotated Passover Haggadah'
(Global Center for Religious Research, Denver, CO, 2021)
Pages 41-90, 141-150

Guggenheimer, Heinrich
'The Scholar's Haggadah - Ashkenazi, Sephardi, & Oriental Versions'
(Jason Aronson Inc., Northfield, New Jersey, 1995)
Pages 76-77, 338

Kulp, Joshua
'The Schechter Haggadah - Art, History and Commentary'
(Schechter Institute of Jewish Studies, Jerusalem, 2009)

Backgrounds of the Illustrations used in this Haggadah

Introduction

The haggadah stands out as the most frequently illustrated, or illuminated, religious text within Judaism. Traversing the pages of the Budoff Haggadah are illustrations inspired by historic haggadot. Adding layers of emotion to the seder, each image reminds us of the rich culture of Jewish communities around the world and the centuries of antisemitism that have sought to destroy it. However, those who peer closely at the illuminations and inscriptions of each haggadot will also find evidence of relations between Jews, Christians, and Muslims. Many artists of Jewish texts were Christian, and throughout these haggadot, we see Christian influences and decorative Arabic elements, all while striving to remain within appropriate iconography.

Prato Haggadah, Spain, 1300

There is only one copy of the Prato Haggadah known to exist, and it is partially unfinished—some pages are blank, while others are exquisitely painted and gilded. A 1617 inscription tells us that it was carried to Italy, likely before the Spanish Inquisition. In 1928, the Czech archaeologist Dr. Ludwig Pollak purchased the haggadah. Tragically, Dr. Pollak was deported to Auschwitz; however, the manuscript did find its way to its promised new owner, David Prato, chief rabbi of Rome. The Prato family later sold it to the Jewish Theological Seminary, where it is housed today.

Birds' Head Haggadah, Germany, 1300

The name refers to the unusual bird-like heads given to all Jewish men, women, and children featured. While several other Jewish manuscripts from this time period also contain bird heads, the reason is unknown. For those who enjoy the bird heads, a child-friendly pop-up version is available from Koren Publishers.

Barcelona Haggadah, Spain, 1340

Created in one of the largest Jewish communities in Europe at the time, this haggadah boasts rich pictorial scenes depicting Passover rituals and intriguing animals surrounding very large, legible Hebrew text. This is one of many haggadot that uses symbolism of the hare hunt, a common illustration in European manuscripts. Knowing well what it means to be hunted down, Jewish communities often resonated with the hare, yet the Barcelona Haggadah offers an inversion of the traditional hunting scene. Here, the dog submits to a regal, standing hare.

Sarajevo Haggadah, Spain, 1350

Two coats of arms decorate the first page of this haggadah, indicating that it may have been a wedding gift. Wine stains throughout the pages show that it was well used for many seders. A 1609 inscription confirms that no anti-church rhetoric was found. During World War II, Dervis Korkut, the Muslim chief librarian of the National Museum in Sarajevo, protected the haggadah from the Nazis. According to legend, Korkut carried the haggadah to a mountainside Muslim village so that it could be safely hidden in a mosque until the war was over.

Lombard Haggadah, Italy, 1390

This work is believed to have been made in the workshop of Giovannino de Grassi, because of illuminations strikingly similar to de Grassi's *Tacuinum sanitatis*, a medieval handbook on health and agriculture. The *Tacuinum* itself is largely based on an eleventh-century Arab work, *Taqwin al-sihha*, written by Ibn Butlan, a Christian physicist.

Amsterdam Haggadah, Netherlands, 1695

Produced by a Jewish convert, former Christian preacher Abraham bar Jacob, this haggadah has a significant legacy. It is the first to use copper engravings for illustrations, and the first Hebrew book to contain a map of the Holy Land. Many of the illustrations can be traced to inspiration from Matthaeus Merian's engravings in a Protestant Bible.

Passover Haggadah, Germany, 1740

While this haggadah does not have a distinct name, it is known to be illustrated by Jacob ben Judah Leib of Berlin in the provenance of Hamburg and Altona. The image featured from this haggadah is of five Rabbis in Bene Brak who held a seder so long, discussing the Exodus, that their students approached them saying, "Rabbis, the time has come to recite the morning shema."

Darmstadt Pessach Haggadah, Denmark, 1769

In the seventeenth century, King Christian IV welcomed Jews to Denmark. Copenhagen grew to have over a hundred thousand Jews, and it is within this thriving community that Polish immigrant Yehuda Leib ben Eliyya Ha-Cohen wrote and illuminated both the 1769 haggadah, and another a decade later.

Bouton Haggadah, 1870

Decorated by Victor Bouton, a French Jewish scribe and heraldic painter, this haggadah is beautifully illuminated with lapis lazuli and gold floral and geometric patterns that resemble miniature Persian paintings of the Shiraz school in the 16th century. The sole illustration is of five men and two women at a table.